PLANTATIONS PROTESTS PULPITS

LESSONS FROM THE PHASES OF MY LIFE

HARRY BLAKE

Dorpie Books
Washington, D. C.

DORPIE BOOKS
WASHINGTON, D.C.

www.dorpiebooks.com

For more information about special discounts for bulk purchases, please visit our website at www.dorpiebooks.com.

Dorpie Books Speakers Bureau can bring authors to your live event. For more information, or to book an event, visit our website at www.dorpiebooks.com.FIRST

FIRST EDITION

Designed by Meagan Carroll

Author photograph © by Brittany Figaro

Additional cover photo credits: National Archives; Bishop College Archives; and the Blake Family Archives

Manufactured in the United States of America

Library of Congress Cataloging-in-Publication Data is available.

ISBN: 978-0-9996794-1-8 (hardcover)

CONTENTS

Contents

This book is dedicated to my Norma.

PART 1

EARLY YEARS
ON THE
PLANTATION

Lying on a handmade mattress filled with white stuffing from the cotton patch, my mother, Dorothy Avery Blake, willed herself to bring me into the world. Though still a young woman, my conception must've seemed as miraculous as God's blessing of Isaac to Sarah. Miss Doll, as everyone, including her children referred to her, had married at the fertile age of seventeen, yet remained barren for seven years.

And what must my father have been feeling? Ike Blake, otherwise named Isaiah by his folks, had already lost his first wife and child during a birth and had likely resigned himself to not ever being a father. Whatever he was feeling—excitement or terror or both—no one would've been the wiser. My father never showed emotion. I once saw an angry white man threaten to kill him —he could've done it too—yet Daddy didn't flinched.

My father was born in Mississippi, but he moved to Portland, Arkansas after the death of his first wife. A white man there had leased about 100 acres of land to a black man, my grandfather Dave Avery, whose children and children's children worked on the land. Daddy joined them in toiling those sun-beaten fields, and in 1927, he joined one of the black overseer's daughters in marriage. I was born there in 1934. Our little family eventually moved nineteen miles away to Lake Village, Arkansas where Daddy worked as a tenant farmer on the Leland Plantation.

What a pair they were! Daddy was several inches shorter than the average man but stood tall in his burly frame. Miss Doll was nearly as tall and strong. My mother had grownup a tomboy and enjoyed working the fields. She wore her hair parted down the center; eyes gray like a wild storm as she faced work with a beaming grin that, eventually, would be accentuated by several gold teeth.

My mother was very talkative, loquacious, verbose, a real chatterbox if ever there was one. She never stopped talking, always saying more than needed to be said. Meanwhile, my father only said what was necessary, which was often not much after, "Good Morning." In this way, and many others, I'm a blend of the two. I got my mother's sense of humor and my father's sense of business. My mother hugged and kissed me and made me feel important. My father kept my feet on the ground. They gave me balance.

My parents weren't drinkers, but Daddy smoked his entire life. He smoked Camel unfiltered cigarettes then eventually switched to Pall Mall, but he would always cut the filters off before smoking. Miss Doll chewed tobacco and dipped snuff. I followed their example on many things except this. It was effortful enduring the smoke, smell, and sounds that accompanied their puffing and spitting, especially during car rides.

In most instances, they performed traditional roles—Daddy had the final say and earned the bulk of the living while Miss Doll was a homemaker. There were exceptions: Momma was comfortable and competent whenever she was needed to tend the fields and Daddy always went to town to purchase any groceries we needed.

Daddy was slow to anger, a very even-tempered man. He knew how to navigate a scene, make good decisions, think ahead. It was he who taught me survival skills. He taught me how to get people to do what I wanted regardless of their status. My mother gave me people skills. My father gave me discernment on understanding human nature.

Momma was God-fearing. She loved going to church, especially revivals. Miss Doll never took a Psychology course, but she thoroughly understood the nature of people. Often, we would spend hours observing people going about their day on the plantation or in and out of small shops near the town square.

Daddy loved Momma, likewise, Momma loved Daddy. He was king of the castle. I wasn't given dinner until Momma served Daddy his plate. When they had a disagreement, they would go out to the poultry house (from houses) and stay there until the issue was resolved. They never argued in front of me. My mother was as headstrong as they came; she believed what she believed. My father gave her space to express it. He would never argue with her. If he agreed, he would say okay. If he didn't, she knew that was a line she should not cross as they simply were not in unison. They suited each other. Opposites attract, after all. Momma made our daddy a god. In turn, he always honored her.

Being sharecroppers, it was common to move from one plantation to another in an attempt to follow the work. It was at such a time, in 1940, when I was about 7, that the Leland Plantation overseer moved to a plantation in Tallulah, Louisiana and brought a dozen or more black workers with him. It was called the Ashley Plantation and was located in Madison Parish. Ten years later, we moved again to a plantation called Woodspur, located in Dixie, Louisiana, just north of Shreveport.

Woodspur was owned by two brothers, the Hunters. They lived in the city and frequently had a chauffeur drive them to the plantation to observe or inspect it. I cannot recall either one ever speaking to us, but I do recall them throwing bread out of their car windows for the dogs as they passed.

Plantations shared a similar geography. Everything was centered around the big house where the manager or owner lived. The equipment was kept nearest to the house, and the row of tenant houses were farthest away with the church in between.

The house I grew up in was white and comfortably small. As was common on plantations, it had been built for tenants to live in. We furnished it ourselves. Daddy covered its windows and doors with screen mesh to keep the flies out, and the interior wallpaper over its wooden planks provided insulation as well as decoration. Those households who could not afford wallpaper used newspaper or magazine pages. Blacks were very resourceful; nothing was wasted. Even the sacks that carried twenty-five pounds of flour or sugar were reused to make pillowcases, underwear, and dresses.

The house had a front room with a fireplace, which doubled as a bedroom and a sitting room. A second room contained an iron bed frame. There was also a kitchen. Although it lacked cabinets, there was a wood-burning stove, and great meals came from that kitchen!

On the front porch was a swing where Miss Doll and I spent the cool nights talking and taking in the fresh country air. We converted the land behind our house into a garden where we grew beets, cabbages, tomatoes, and all manner of peas. Various nut and fruit trees grew around the garden.

Since we had no bathroom, Daddy built an outhouse (though we referred to it as the privy, since it sounded much nicer). In 1949, electricity was installed on the plantation. It was nice to have convenient light for night reading and study. An electric washing machine, gas heating, and a refrigerator with a freezer to make ice cubes were also nice additions. Before then, we had burned kerosene lamps and used the wood stove to heat the house. Food and milk had been kept cold with the aid of an icebox. Ice blocks would be purchased on weekends from traveling ice salesmen.

As a child, I gathered eggs, fed hogs, and pumped water. I also chopped and sawed firewood into pieces that could fit in the stove then stacked the wood into a pile. During harvest, I picked wild berries and gathered ears of corn, tomatoes, peas, and other crops. I erected and tore down fences. Baling and stacking hay were also some of my obligations. Eventually, I was lifting hundred pound bales of hay. I was always small, but over time I became strong and muscular. At the tender age of 12, chopping cotton was added to my repertoire.

By my teenage years, there was no task on the plantation I couldn't do. One of my jobs, which I didn't care for but came with great responsibility, was driving the mules. I'd hitch two mules to planters carrying containers I'd filled with seeds. As the mules walked, the seeds dropped into the soil where they would sprout into proud crops.

Depending on the task, twenty to a hundred people worked in the fields. To distract from the labor and pass the time, they laughed and joked as they told stories and talked about life. The conversations were really interesting, not idle talk. People with good voices graced us with spiritual songs and some blues.

When tenants had harvested the crops and sold their half, their rent and other expenses, such as the use and care of the mules and farm implements likes plows, weed cutters, planters, and cultivators would be deducted from their remaining proceeds. Many tenants were never able to get out of debt. On top of that, sharecroppers who owed the plantation money risked getting killed if they left. Though the time of tree lynchings had passed, white folks were not beyond throwing a black man into the river or dragging him behind a horse or truck. Other than sneaking out under the cover of darkness, the only way indebted blacks could escape was to be bought by another plantation owner. It was, for all intents and purposes, a form of slavery.

Many tenants had side businesses. Women would be seamstresses and men would farm their own tiny plots; Daddy was one of these people. In addition to the hogs he raised, he built a chicken coop and a smokehouse to sell fryers, as well as bacon, ham, and other cured meats. He made more money from his small farm than he did on the plantation. His financial fortune was compounded by his thrift; another man's trash was his treasure. If he found some iron or tin in the street, for example, he took it to the junkyard and sold it. As a result, Daddy always had money and plenty of food for us to share.

SCHOOL YEARS

Daddy only worked for landowners who believed in taking decent care of their black employees. This included having a church on the plantation that doubled as a schoolhouse where the thirty or so school-age children gathered to learn from a teacher chosen by the plantation owner. The books that students received to use were hand-me-downs from white schools. It seemed very likely that certain pages were deliberately torn out of the text books.

The school year was split to accommodate planting and harvesting seasons. We mostly attended school during the winter months though we'd often take some days off in November and December to pick ripe pecans. The plantation teacher, Minnie E. W. Kuntz, had been a student at Southern University, the historically black college in Louisiana, and at that time, the largest black college. She introduced us to the inventor George Washington Carver, as well as Tuskegee Institute founder, Booker T. Washington. She was inspirational, but the task of teaching all subjects to students in first through seventh grades was impossible, even with the older kids tutoring the younger children. As a consequence,

I was almost a teenager by the time I could competently read and write.

Once I reached eighth grade, Daddy got me a driving exception, so I could use the car to get to middle school ten miles away in Tallulah. The other students had attended city schools all along and seemed impossibly far ahead of me, so I had a very difficult time. I did not know what a fraction was nor had I ever heard of the parts of speech. For the first time in my life, I realized I was playing catch-up.

Understandably, I was overwhelmed. Yet, I couldn't let that consume me. Had it been up to Momma, whose education had ended in the third grade, I would not have had to go to school. She'd have prefered having her playmate home with her anyway (she was very easy on me), but it wasn't up to her. Daddy insisted I get an education even though (or perhaps because) he was illiterate.

I would study all night while asking God to help me. On some nights, I found myself crying until sleep embraced me. I started buying self-help books on speed reading and how to read in general, which was when I discovered the source of my dilemmas. I had a learning disability called dyslexia, that is, I reversed my letters which made reading difficult. Even though I had not yet conquered it, merely understanding my problem provided immediate relief.

One thing I was determined to master was grammar so I could be as fluent, if not more so, than white people. I had seen white people laugh at the way black people talked. Whenever they laughed at Daddy, I thought to myself, *You may laugh at me, but it won't be for the way I talk.*

In the spring of 1951, I began attending Booker T. Washington High School in Shreveport. Named for the pioneering black educator, the high school was commissioned to address the overcrowded, deplorable conditions at Shreveport's Central Colored High School. The new school was the envy of other black high schools and even of the white folks. When it opened in 1950, it was featured in LIFE magazine and hailed for its innovative architecture, rigorous academic programs, and educational programs for technical and industrial sectors such as printing, cosmetology, dry cleaning, as well as for other careers. Nearly every kind of trade school had a program there.

As it happened, I eventually became a leader at the school. Even with a slate of female candidates, I was elected president of our student body, a class of over four hundred. I still do not understand how a country boy raised on a plantation with a one-room schoolhouse became the president of a group of city kids, but to this day, I am exceedingly proud of and humbled by the opportunity.

While I was at Booker T. Washington, a political awakening was happening among the students; the required reading included books by revolutionary thinkers such as W. E. B. DuBois, Frederick Douglass, and a young preacher named Martin Luther King, Jr. I had heard talk on the plantation about a movement starting in America, led by people like Dr. King. Now I was reading about it in the local black newspaper, the Shreveport Sun, as well as the Pittsburgh Courier, a national black newspaper, fifty copies of which I sold every week to folks on the plantation.

On my drives to school and back, I perceived the notion to look for a summer job off the plantation, one indoors with air conditioning if I could finagle it! In the summer of 1951, I went job-hunting at the country store, a building about the size of a large bedroom. The white owner said to me, "No, boy. I don't need anybody. I just hired two summer helpers, one from Grambling and one from Tech."

I remember thinking to myself, *This white man must be a pretty decent employer. He has gone and hired a black college student AND a white college student.* This made him an equal opportunity employer long before such practices supposedly became common. Indeed, the owner, Hustler Lloyd "H. L." Whitlow, turned out to be what some white folks dubbed a "nigger lover." An unusual act of kindness, he sold groceries to blacks on credit. Field hands and domestic workers were allowed to pay their grocery bills when they received their wages at the end of each week, and elderly on pensions could pay when they got their checks at the beginning of each month. A retired Army officer, Mr. Whitlow was raised by parents sympathetic to the plight of blacks. Unlike most whites at that time, he genuinely wanted racial equality. He was very optimistic, too, particularly about the future. He often said to me, "Things are going to change, this is just how it is now. But just you wait..."

As luck would have it, Mrs. Whitlow happened to be outside when her husband Mr. Whitlow shooed me away. My greeting led to a conversation which led to her saying, "I like you. I'm going to get my husband to hire you."

Shortly thereafter, Whitlow told me, "Okay, day laborers come in to buy sandwiches at around 6 a.m., so you best be here no later than 5:30, and don't ask me what I'm going to pay you."

I assumed I'd be making more than I had on the plantation where I could work five days a week for three dollars a day. At the store, I was going to work six days. I was excited! That is until the end of the week when Mr. Whitlow told me he shared his wife's affinity for me and would show it by paying me fifteen dollars a week.

I considered that very briefly before determining that I could make that much on the plantation working less hours. While finishing my work, I thought about how to handle this. Finally, I said to Mr. Whitlow, "Well, sir, if this is all you think I'm worth, I'll just donate this fifteen dollars back to you this week."

A little indignant, he asked, "Well, hell. What do you think you're worth?"

I replied, "Well, you can't pay me what I'm worth, but I couldn't take less than twenty-five dollars."

He tossed it at me, but I got my twenty-five dollars! Later, when school started, Mr. Whitlow got sick, and his wife asked Daddy if I could drive over to work before and after school. They then had to pay me more than twenty-five dollars a week, and eventually, I earned more the following summer when I worked there full time. By the time I graduated from high school, I was making three hundred dollars a month. No black man on a tractor made that much money anywhere. Mr. Whitlow impacted my life more than any other man except my daddy.

There were a lot of decent white folks, but they were usually afraid to show kindness to blacks in public. They typically treated us more like pets than equals. For instance, a plantation owner who liked a particular worker would tell that worker something like, "Stay out of the cemetery, and I'll keep you out of jail." Such blacks were protected no matter what they did, unless they did it to a white person—no one was crazy enough to attempt that.

Where I grew up, most of the plantation owners were decent white folks. When tenants died, their owners wept. They treated workers as they would family. If a worker got sick, the plantation owner would get them a doctor. If a tenant needed a car, the owner would secure a loan for them. Laborers considered too valuable for plantation owners to lose were also kept from being drafted into the military by intervening on the draft board.

This was, of course, as it should have been considering black people were the most valuable commodities on a plantation. Black folks raised their children and cooked their meals. So yes, white folks would do anything to help black people as long as it did not put them in disfavor within their white circles. To this day, the general attitude toward blacks continued to be mostly paternalistic.

As graduation approached in 1954, my high school counselor, Hazel Payne whom I always referred to as Ms. Payne even after she became Mrs. Phillips, changed the course of my life with one question: "Harry, where are you going to college?"

Ms. Payne, one of the original counselors at the Booker T. Washington, was utterly devoted to her students, having not yet had any children of her own. I knew her to be a kind and excellent teacher. Years later, when I was affiliated with New Boggy Baptist Church where her grandfather pastored and she worshipped, I also came to know of her deep, abiding faith. I cherished her to the day she died at about the age of ninety-five, not many years ago.

In answer to her question, I explained that I knew about Howard University, and of course, Tuskegee Institute. I then told her how much I would have liked to attend Morehouse College had I had enough money.

She replied, "My grandfather, who lives in Marshall, Texas, boards university students in his house, and I want you to meet him."

And so the course of my education was steered toward Bishop College where Ms. Payne's sister and brother were educators.

Ms. Payne's grandfather, Dr. Samuel Howard, was the pastor of New Boggy Baptist Church, so an added perk of staying at his house was the opportunity to study under his pastoral tutelage. A mild-mannered man, he was definitely not of the whooping tradition. He had pastored two churches simultaneously before New Boggy, and his exemplary life was held in high regard. Little did I know at the time that I would succeed him as pastor. After meeting Dr. Howard, I was sent to meet with the president of Bishop College. He was known as Dr. M. K. Curry.

Having explained that I had just graduated from Booker T. Washington and wanted to attend Bishop, I told him, "I don't have any money, but I do know how to work."

His reply to that was a simple yet life-changing, "If you can work, I'll see you when school starts in September."

BISHOP
COLLEGE

Upon my arrival at Bishop College, Dr. Curry assigned me to his wife. Mrs. Marjorie Curry managed the student center where she put me to work as a short-order cook. At the center, I served sandwiches, hamburgers, sodas, and ice cream sundaes to the students every afternoon.

I remember that time as if it were yesterday. As I pursued my major in religious studies and minor in English, I attended classes from 8:00 a.m to 11:00 a.m. and worked from noon to 5:00 p.m. I worked so many hours that Bishop College owed me money when I graduated! Suffice to say, every now and then I was fond of teasing the Currys that they never paid me what the college owed me for my work.

Both of the Currys were people of great faith. Dr. Curry made a sacrifice for the future of the establishment. He gave up his pastorate to become the president of Bishop College. Aiming to lead the college from its glory days, he literally moved Bishop College, transporting everything but the buildings on trucks from Marshall to Dallas, Texas, where it became a powerhouse from 1961 to 1985.

Primarily a seminary, Bishop College was founded by the Baptist Home Mission Society in 1881 for the purpose of providing a college for African American Baptists. The effort was led by Nathan Bishop, who had been the superintendent of several major school systems in New England.

My time at Bishop College was quite enjoyable. I became president of the Bishop College Lyceum, an organization for clergy students, and also helped to charter the Mu Gamma chapter of Omega Psi Phi Fraternity, Inc. on campus in 1957. Productivity was no stranger to one who grew up working. I also had the opportunity to meet with some of the nation's greatest minds, such as Dr. Harold Thompson, a professor of philosophy of religion, and his successor, Dr. Richard A. Rollins, a man who particularly influenced me.

Dr. King was my commencement speaker in 1959. It was an exciting time to be in college; young people were leading what was quickly becoming a nationwide Civil Rights Movement. Although the Movement started in Montgomery, Alabama, Dr. Vernon Johns, King's mentor and predecessor as pastor of Dexter Avenue Baptist Church, was unable to galvanize people the way Dr. King could.

My introduction to Dr. King was spurred on by the father of the Civil Rights Movement who happened to live in Shreveport. We were personally introduced thanks to Dr. C. O. Simpkins. He was a local dentist and a charter member of the Southern Christian Leadership Conference (SCLC), which was founded in Louisiana at the New Zion Baptist Church in New Orleans where his fellow charter member Dr. A. L. Davis was a pastor. Louisiana was very influential in the Civil Rights Movement. These two men helped to establish the SCLC, together with Dr. Theodore Judson Jemison, former president of the National Baptist Convention USA, Inc.

I was recommended by Dr. Simpkins to Dr. King for a job as a field representative in the Shreveport area, in which I would register black people to vote as well as conduct voter education. Of course, I was excited about this opportunity. However, before accepting I sought the support of my parents who I knew would be in harm's way if any consequences were to follow. My daddy's answer was a bolster of encouragement, in his own personal way. Daddy said he would be disappointed if I turned the offer down. Since he ventured from the plantation much more than Momma did, he was subsequently harassed by the police.

Whenever he was driving somewhere, they stopped him along the road, calling him stupid or a nigger. Their intimidation tactics were meant to pressure me into submission. I was always so appreciative and proud of the way my family, especially my wife, withstood the resulting pressures.

They were the strongest people I knew.

FAMILY
EXPANSION

My life changed dramatically during high school when my brother Herman Blake was born 17 years after me. I was just getting used to having Herman around when Robert was born almost a year later. It was as if my parents were compensating for taking so long to have more children. In 1953, my parents finally had a little girl. Momma used to pretend we boys were all she wanted. When I picked her and my baby sister up from the hospital, she teasingly said, "I don't have no use for a girl," to which I quipped, "Well then, can I take her home and name her Carolyn?"

I did not spend much time with my siblings after I went off to college, but as they grew up, they revered me like a second father. Since I worked, I could buy them things my parents could not afford. Not only did this include toys and treats, but also books and other educational materials. I take pride in their academic accomplishments; all my siblings have college degrees and my sister acquired a master's degree.

I met Norma at the New Boggy Baptist Church in Bethany, Louisiana. Her family had been longtime members. Pastor Howard was the one who baptized her, and she always declared him to be her only pastor. We had gone to high school together, but she had been a freshman and I a busy senior, so our paths had never crossed (though she swore she had always had her eye on me!). One of the deacons at the church had his eye on me for his daughter, but I only had eyes for Norma, drawn to her compassionate spirit and beautiful complexion. When I proposed to her, I was so poor that I could not even afford an engagement ring. I had offered her my fraternity pin instead. She took that pin as if it was the same value as a fancy ring. On August 31, 1958, a year before I graduated from Bishop, Norma became my wife and my partner for life.

Shortly after graduating, I took up a job as a baker's helper, in which I weighed, measured, and mixed ingredients. Despite paying good money ($192 weekly), I felt restless. I had told Norma about my desire to be an agent of change, which is why when Dr. King offered me the position of field representative for SCLC's Northern Louisiana territory, Norma gave me her blessing and threw her full support behind me. I started on March 1, 1960. It may have paid only $75 weekly, but the value it added to my life was worth much more. It was a time of excitement and a highlight of all my years. I enjoyed every second of it!

ACTIVISM AND THE CIVIL RIGHTS MOVEMENT

he sit-ins had begun a few months before I joined as staff of SCLC. The first lunch counter demonstration was in Raleigh, North Carolina; such demonstrations were mainly in places with black colleges and universities. College students always led these efforts since they had no children or jobs and, therefore, could most afford the risks involved. Dr. C. O. Simpkins and I set about organizing voting rights protests all over the state, including at Southern University, which at the time was the largest black university in the world. It is often overlooked by many that even black institutions had complicated allegiances, particularly black universities funded by white state legislatures. We put even the president of Southern University, the iconic Dr. Felton G. Clark, who was very influential among white folks, in a pickle. He was pelted by words like "You can't control your niggers? They out here protesting?"

Student leaders were banished from every college in the state. One such leader was Donald Moss, a man who came from a family of educators but never finished college in Louisiana. Calvin

Austin was expelled from Booker T. Washington and was not allowed to attend any school in Caddo Parish (50 years later, Caddo Parish gave him an honorary diploma). Dr. Clark himself sacrificed a few student leaders for what he believed was the greater good of educating blacks.

The protests were part of my efforts to convince blacks to become registered voters, which was a very difficult process. Louisiana law stated that a person registering to vote had to be recommended by someone who was already registered. If no blacks were registered, then who was going to recommend black people? Only a few decent white people were willing to do that. After the recommendation, applicants had to be able to interpret any portion of the Constitution to the satisfaction of the registrar. If an applicant failed the registrar's quiz, the only recourse was to take it again. Throughout this process, blacks suffered countless indignities. The struggle and humiliation dug deep. A vast majority were spat on, snitched about, or forced to wait for hours even if there was no one was in front of them. But before any of that, I had to convince black folks of the importance of voting—that because it was relevant to their lives, they needed to exercise their rights. Back then, there were 300,000 white voters and only 5,000 black voters in the state, so that it seemed to make no difference. The fact that one had to wait for an election also diminished its effectiveness in the eyes of blacks. Still, my fellow activists and I knew that increasing the black vote was essential for changing the system. However, black people did not see the impact of their votes until that fateful day when they helped elect President John F. Kennedy.

In contrast, the sit-ins and store demonstrations had an immediate impact. Injustice was tangible and immediate. Blacks could see and feel the unfairness of the fancy local stores, where they were not allowed to try on clothes and had to use bathrooms in the basement instead of on the main floor.

My work as an activist was focused primarily on North Louisiana and East Texas, but I went and was willing to go wherever Dr. King needed me.

Although I greatly admired Dr. King and cherished our relationship, it never dawned on me to take a photo with him for posterity's sake. I never liked to take pictures, in general. I still have not figured out how to smile, though I do know how to laugh. I had a sense of humor and so did Dr. King. I remember how he loved to tease the waitresses when we ate at the Freeman and Harris Restaurant. When ordering breakfast, Dr. King would humorously request, "Virginia, I need a lot a sense today, so scramble me some eggs with brains and bacon and dried toast."

The joke referred to the pig brains from the hog's head that was apparently considered a delicacy.

In 1961, Dr. King held the SCLC in Shreveport. I was the coordinator, and the keynote speaker was Dr. Benjamin Mays, the president of Morehouse College. Our meetings were held in churches and attended by about 500 activists from across the South. Few locals attended the conference. They appeared justifiably hesitant. Most of the participants were college students since they had less at stake. Older adults did what they could. They contributed in their own ways, telling us things like, "Here's a $10, but mind you, I don't want to hear my name mentioned."

In some instances they would give us as much as $50. In those cases, they probably had tricked the white folks into giving them the money. We were constantly under surveillance. The police department planted bugs in churches and businesses of known activists. Black informants were recruited to wear recording devices when they attended our meetings. It was not an overstatement to state that the police commissioner was pure evil. George Wendell D'Artois Sr. had those recordings transcribed, figured out who had attended the meetings, or who spoke at the rally. He used this information to pressure their employers to get rid of them. Those who worked for Caddo Parish School Board were immediately fired. In one case, a police officer told the school superintendent which teachers had attended. All that was said was a mere, "You need to do something about it," and just like that their jobs were a thing of the past. The same thing happened to blacks who worked as maids or chauffeurs. In this way, black folks in Shreveport were terrorized. Fear was the method used to keep them under control. For nearly a century, whites in Caddo Parish had also been violent against black citizens. There was a history of it. More lynchings had taken place in what became known as "Bloody" Caddo Parish than almost anywhere else in the country. White mobs had carried out sanctioned lynchings on courthouse grounds, using a Southern live oak tree donated by Judge Thomas Fletcher Bell.

When Dr. King saw that the police had already arrived wherever he went, he was rumored to have said, "There are some peculiar black folks in Shreveport."

Shreveport was different from King's hometown of Atlanta, or even Birmingham, in that there was very little industrial work.

Black residents of Shreveport had a plantation mentality because it was quite literally a plantation community; as a consequence, when white people told them things like, "Don't get mixed up with them niggers over there. I been good to you. Stay out of trouble." they quickly responded, "Yes, sa" and even walked on the other side of the street to avoid people like me. Everything was polite on the surface. They could keep their jobs if they stayed in line.

Professions such as barbers, beauticians, undertakers, and black pastors had a bit more freedom. Since I was not employed by a white person, I did not have to worry about losing my livelihood. But there was another reason the police could not control me: Daddy had trained me all my life never to fear white people or what they could do to me. My faith in the cause was fervent and so was my decision, my resolve, to stand against evil. To me, there was nothing to lose. If I lived, I was living for God; if I died, I was going to be with him. Not everybody had that kind of commitment, and I do not condemn them for it. After a while, though, the burdens of the Civil Rights Movement began weighing heavily on me. The year 1963 was full of ups and downs. I had been elected president of the National Association of American Colored People (NAACP) chapter in Shreveport, which sent me and Ann Brewster to the nation's capital for the March on Washington on August 27. I do not think anybody expected the event to be so impactful nor could I have predicted that so many people would be there. There had never been a march this large. On top of it all, it was peaceful. The people who organized it were brilliant. It was a moment of great celebration, one of the shining highlights of my life. Yet only a month later, I experienced one of the lowest points in my life.

On September 15, 1963, Ku Klux Klan members planted a bomb in 16th Street Baptist Church in Birmingham, killing four innocent black girls in the explosion. Our local NAACP chapter organized a march during the following week to memorialize the children who had died. I asked for a permit the Monday before Sunday's march, but the commissioner waited until noon on Saturday to respond. When he denied it, I said, "Commissioner, you had a week to make your decision. You're only giving me six seconds? There is not time to cancel it."

"Anyone in the march will get arrested" was his reply, and he was known to be a man of his word.

To mitigate the situation, I called a board meeting, where we decided to assemble at Little Union Baptist Church instead. But we still had to get people out of the church after the service ended. I looked outside from the church vestibule and saw what seemed like hundreds of police officers stopping and questioning all the black drivers in a manner that seemed like rough interrogation. Even those in cars with out-of-state license plates were not overlooked. The police even shocked black people with cow prods as they were standing on their front porches. A lawyer named Jessie Stone went out to the commissioner, telling him that the memorial service was over and that the people needed to come out; to that, the commissioner instructed that they come out two by two. As I was watching this, a police officer attacked me with his iron grip and pulled me out of the church; then every officer who could get near me beat me. I was left seemingly lifeless on the ground.

Norma refused to allow me to be taken to a local hospital. She feared the whites might finish me off. Instead, I was taken to the home of a Pastor Walter A. Jones of Mt. Chapel Baptist Church in nearby Mooretown. Jones declared that any police who tried to retrieve me from his home would be dead police. Mrs. Maxine Sarpy, who was a nurse, administered first aid to me in the pastor's study. The next day, Norma and I flew to Dallas, where I stayed in the hospital for over a week.

Once we knew I would be okay, I found the heart to summon my sense of humor. I joked that if they were trying to kill me, Momma could have told them they had made a mistake by choosing to hit my head, the hardest part of my body. After I was released from the hospital, my wife and I stayed in the adult housing at Bishop College. It was during that time when I reflected on everything that had transpired.

Back in Shreveport, on the Monday following my beating, the black youth protested at the high school and the junior high school because they felt something happening, the ripple in the pond was in motion. The students were tear gassed and beaten when they started marching. Police struck one of the black assistant principals and a black female teacher on the campus of Booker T. Washington. Aside from them, no one in the Movement rallied to support me; not a single organization issued a statement. Even though we had proof that law enforcement had nearly killed me, the national NAACP declined to take my case because they had committed all their funds to lawsuits in Birmingham and other cities more closely associated with the Movement. Though I have been hesitant to acknowledge it, this angered me immensely. I felt wronged, if not even a bit betrayed. Over the next few years, the fervor of the Movement also died down.

In 1964, the Civil Rights Act passed, outlawing discrimination based on race; the Voting Rights Act passed in the following year, prohibiting racial discrimination in voter registration. Since this was what we had been fighting for, the emotional intensity dissipated, though we knew there was still work to be done. The lunch counter demonstrations and boycotts receded into the clutches of time gone by. For me and many others, the Movement we knew died on a balcony in Memphis, Tennessee. I was preaching a revival in Muskegon, Michigan, for Pastor Wyatt L. Stewart, who had been a fellow activist in Shreveport. His brother had pastored Galilee, the first church that Dr. King ever preached at in Shreveport. Just as I approached the pulpit, I was handed a note stating that Dr King had been assassinated. It should not have been a major shock as all activists lived with that threat looming over their heads. In fact, Dr. King himself had even alluded to this in his speech the night before when he had said, "I've been to the mountaintop, but I may not get there with you."

Though this moment had seemed inevitable, I was stunned and devastated nonetheless. Heartbroken, I was in a daze for much of that week. After I returned home, my wife, her grandmother, Savannah Jernigan, and I flew to Atlanta for the funeral held at Ebenezer Baptist Church, where both Dr. King and his father had pastored. Though I was no longer on the staff of the SCLC, having transitioned to full-time pastoring, I still helped out from time to time. Much of the talk there centered around the question: How do we continue to realize Dr. King's dream, every black person's dream?

A sense of foreboding was welling up. We were also worried about what was to come. Many black people felt trapped, helpless. This state of not knowing what to do lead to the riots, in which the desperate folks burned down their cities to get the attention of society.

Rioting was never meant to be part of the Movement. The erupting violence marred Dr. King's methods, and many cities erred. I grieved that people did the very thing Dr. King had spoken against. We were to be peaceful. On that note, pastors took the initiative to calm those perpetrating the riots, with the intention of restoring peace and direction.

THE MINISTRY

he Church had been a part of my life since before I can remember. Every plantation I lived on had a church built by the owner; on one of them, there was both a Methodist and a Baptist church. My momma was a very active church member, beloved by the entire congregation.

By the time I was five, I could understand what church was about and looked forward to attending. I remember one time when Momma decided to leave me at home with Daddy while she attended a revival. Younger me was having none of that; I was determined to go with her. I snatched a freshly washed and starched pair of overalls from the clothesline, put them on, and walked the mile to church. Miss Doll was certainly not the most impressed to see her son shoeless in unironed overalls, but she got the message that I wanted to attend revivals too.

At about the age of twelve, I accepted Jesus Christ as my lord and personal savior while attending a revival at Jerusalem Baptist Church on the Ashley Plantation. I was baptized by Pastor Garfield Israel, who simultaneously pastored four churches. Back then, a pastor's preaching skills were judged by the number of churches he led simultaneously. A pastor who had only one church was considered nearly a jackleg preacher, whereas a pastor who presided over four churches concurrently was considered a good preacher. Some even preached at two or more churches per Sunday. Baptisms were performed on the bank of a pond or a bayou on Sunday mornings with the whole congregation gathered. Women donned their wide-brimmed hats or brought parasols to shield themselves from the hot sun. Either the pastor, a deacon, or a deaconess would begin singing an old spiritual began like "Take me to the water, take me to the water, take me to the water, to be baptized..."

Soon, the individual voices of the congregation joined in chorus as they sang along. The pastor then baptized someone with each pause in the song.

After I was baptized, I joined Momma's church, Pleasant Hill Baptist Church, which was just outside the city limits of Tallulah. I was a member there from 1946 to December 1950. I then became a member of The Rose of Sharon Baptist Church on the Woodspur plantation in Dixie, Louisiana, pastored by Reverend C. L. Pennywell. There I stayed until it was time to leave the Woodspur plantation and move to Shreveport.

When I graduated from high school, my boss, H. L. Whitlow, had his church offer me a scholarship to Stillman College in Tuscaloosa, Alabama, which had been founded by the Presbyterian Church. Although grateful for this gesture, I turned it down as I felt the school might pressure me to become a Presbyterian minister. I was fully committed to the Baptist denomination, so I chose to work my way through Bishop College instead.

While in college, I drove 45 minutes back home to work on the plantation all day on Saturdays and attend my church on Sundays. At one point, I took a year off from college to determine whether I should accept a calling to the ministry. Nice, well-spoken young black men were often told, "You go'n' be a preacher." Knowing that, I wanted to make sure my calling was from God and not from the people who had said that to me throughout my life.

I also did not want to be led by my ego; pastors had a very high status in the black community, and I knew that I could serve the Church in other ways, having served as a Sunday school teacher and been appointed a deacon at age 16. In 1956, I discerned that it was not the will of man nor my ego beckoning me. I was, in fact, being called by God. I accepted my calling and went back to college.

The college I attended trained me not only for the ministry, but also for much of my activist work as an officer in the SCLC. However, even while serving as a leader of the local Civil Rights Movement, I dedicated time to pastor small black churches that met only once or twice a month.

One of them was Elizabeth Baptist Church, a rural church in a little North Caddo Parish community called Belcher, where I served as pastor from 1958 to 1962. Though I had never actually attended the church before becoming pastor, I was close friends with its previous pastor, Rev. C. L. Townsel, who was also a graduate of Bishop College. Pastor Townsel had previously pastored the Mt. Calm Baptist Church of Minden and was at that time leaving Elizabeth to pastor Morning Star Missionary Baptist Church in

Shreveport. By the time he died prematurely at about 60 years of age, he had already forged a great legacy there.

Elizabeth had about 100 names on the rolls, with 50 members in regular attendance. Its members were familiar with me from my work at Whitlow's store.

Some of them were businesspeople, but most were landowners (though it was a farming community, they did not call themselves farmers because it reminded them too much of plantations). All of them owned their own homes, and some of them were quite well-off as for as money was concerned.

The congregation typically met once a month on Sundays. Looking back, I cannot claim I did anything earthshaking at Elizabeth. The most notable things I did there were teaching social skills to the youth and replacing the church benches with pews.

After New Boggy's pastor, Dr. Samuel Howard, retired in 1959, I was delighted when my name was presented as a candidate to succeed him. Though, in truth, the deacons did not want me as pastor, primarily because I had not married into the family of their choice. New Boggy had about 1,200 members on the rolls and 300 in regular attendance. I served there from April 1960 to September 1966.

Although I was fond of all my churches, New Boggy held a special place in my heart because that is where I found my soulmate, Norma. I also greatly appreciated Dr. Howard for making it possible for me to attend Bishop College by providing free room and board during my college years. I loved him dearly. Another reason for my high regard was due to New Boggy's rich history.

Under the leadership of one of its most prominent pastors, Reverend A. M. Moore, the church had constructed and established an academy. Interestingly enough, the good Reverend had a brother who was a prominent citizen of Shreveport for whom Mooretown was named. The sanctuary, which seated 800, was probably 100 years old; it even had indoor restrooms though the outdoor privy had not been torn down because older members refused to use the indoor facilities. I think they thought it was a sin to use a bathroom in a church. At one time, the church had also had an academy with a dormitory each for boys, girls, and a faculty of as many as 18 teachers and a principal.

New Boggy opened my eyes to the endless possibilities of black wealth and independence. For many decades, the congregation had been operating gas and oil wells that produced a great income for the church. The church also had a group that managed its very large cemetery as well as the land. Imagine a congregation with that kind of vision in the 1800s!

In March 1961, I also began pastoring Lake Bethlehem Baptist Church in a densely populated black neighborhood called Cooper Road, Louisiana. It has since been renamed in honor of Dr. King. Founded in the late 1920s, it remains one of the oldest continuous black communities. Cooper Road was the first neighborhood encountered by blacks migrating from rural towns north of Shreveport such as Oil City, Dixie, and Belcher. It had thriving black-owned grocery stores, wonderful restaurants, and anything else citizens needed; however, it was still very rural in that the streets were unpaved and there was no sewage system.

By 1966, I was unable to continue at both churches because I had led them to become full-time churches. Rather than choose between two churches that I dearly loved, inevitably leaving one flock feeling hurt and rejected, I accepted an assignment at my beloved Mount Canaan Baptist Church. I should mention that I had been considered for the pastorate there in 1961, but passed over for fear that my involvement in the Movement would be dangerous to the church. Since I had resigned from the NAACP and the SCLC, such concerns had diminished.

When I started at Mount Canaan, there were between 400 and 500 members on the rolls. The dilapidated building appeared to be the home of pigeons. The leaks in the roof were also a cause for concern. Rather than pews, the congregation sat on benches built by church members. Mount Canaan was located in the Allendale neighborhood. At the time, it was the most densely populated black community in Shreveport. Though a few were homeowners, most people there were renting shotgun houses, over 60 of which had to be bought and demolished in order to build where the church currently stands.

Although Mount Canaan had neglected its church building, for an establishment in the 1940s and '50s the church had been ahead of its time in other ways. I think the previous pastor, Dr. A. S. Jackson, had been far more learned than I am. The congregation was highly educated and even had a bookstore. The choir was second to none—and I cannot stress enough the importance of having a good choir in a Baptist church! They did a Sunday evening broadcast that was standing room only. However, the church was surrounded by tenants living in shacks and shotgun houses. Some people still had outdoor toilets!

We could simply not just be sophisticated inside the building; I knew we had to do something for the community, and so we did. As I read the Scriptures, I realized that when Jesus preached, he did not require people to come to him; rather, he went to them wherever they were. Whether in the streets or on the mountains, masses of people followed him. If he could do it, so could I! Perhaps he was even modeling what modern-day churches should be doing; after all, people receive the truth when it is spoken to them in love.

Thus, I took the initiative. Inspired by the Scriptures, I began preaching in the streets. The choir and I picked a block where we asked someone to let us plug in an amplifier with an extension cord. We used a microphone with speakers to minister from the back of a pickup truck. We would start with singing and praying, then I made my appeal. Many people accepted Christ; half of them were drunkards who then sobered up.

But we did not just give people the gospel. We also built low-income housing in Allendale for 120 families. When I started as pastor, I believe three kids graduated from high school; at the height of my tenure, we had more college and graduate students completing degrees than the 15 to 20 students receiving high school diplomas.

In the 1970s, we started a tutorial program. We were also the first church to provide free meals for children during the summer. Caddo Parish, watching our actions, then took over that program. 1976 was the year in which we built a new sanctuary.

PASTORAL BROTHER-HOOD

When I first moved to Shreveport, I bonded with two pastors who would remain my closest friends. Across the city, we became known as the Trio of pastoral leaders. One of them, Dr. E. Edward Jones, was the young pastor of Galilee Baptist Church, the mother to Mount Canaan, which it established as a mission church. Black Baptists usually created churches through splitting off congregations, but not in this case. In late 1959, Jones invited me to preach at Galilee, and thus our friendship began.

Jones was reared in a different city. He was a distinguished graduate of Grambling University, and later, Bishop College's School of Religion. A great leader and administrator, he accomplished phenomenal things at Galilee. Years after his death, his legacy still remains. Galilee built a 39-acre gated community and other industrial and housing developments, including two designed specifically for the elderly and the handicapped. Mount Canaan members all too gladly helped Galilee obtain funds for one of its building projects.

Jones was also a supporter of Dr. King and invited him to speak at Galilee whenever Dr. King was in town. This was a stark contrast to some who thought it was too dangerous to let Dr. King visit their churches. There were several churches in Shreveport that openly supported Dr. King, namely Galilee, Evergreen, and Little Union. Galilee became the headquarters of Dr. King's activist efforts in the Shreveport area.

An activist himself, Jones filed suit to integrate one of the elementary schools in Shreveport; as a result, the school opened its doors to his children, as well as to other black students in the locality. While I do not recall Jones occupying any political positions, he did get others elected through his influence and with his efforts to hold people accountable to the law. At one point, for example, his wife, Leslie Jones, was appointed to serve in an unexpired seat on the local school board. Jones held local and state leadership positions within the Baptist denomination before becoming president of the National Baptist Convention of America, Inc. (NBC), which at the time had over two-million members. Ebony magazine named him one of the 100 most influential black men in America. A man who exuded friendliness, Jones had an amazing memory for names and faces. An example of this occurred at a convention of between three and four thousand people where he could recall everyone's names.

Jones and I often had informal meetings in which we had lunch together. Sometimes, I visited him at his office, as I felt it too much of an imposition to have the pastor of the mother church visit me. When I stopped by his office one Christmas Eve, I ate some fruit he had with him. As I bit into an apple, my dentures fractured. Even worse, the dental office was closed. I told him I would never again eat anything he offered me.

During these meetings, information was exchanged and confidence was built. We shared with each other the innovative things we were doing at our churches. I told Jones about a program I had established that increased prayer-meeting attendance at Mount Canaan from a high of 18 in August 1979 to a high of 665. He was startled to hear that there was an average of 405 per week by the end of 1984. Impressed, he then catapulted me to the national stage, inviting me to present my model for that program before hundreds of pastors at the institutions he led.

My other friend, Dr. Brady L. Blade, and I went to high school together, though I did not get to know him then because he was a freshman during my senior year. Pastor Blade was a boy preacher who left Shreveport to finish high school and go to college in Texas. I kept hearing about him while I was at New Boggy. When I heard that he had given up his pastorate in West Texas and been called to the Zion Baptist Church, another daughter church of Galilee, I invited him to speak at one of my churches. We hit it off easily.

Pastor Blade and I became close friends. I was privileged that he invited me to preach at his installation service at Zion. More so, when I was asked to preside over his sister's funeral as well. The two of us simply clicked. And so, it was with great honor that I assumed the role as best man at his wedding. While we waited for the bride to come down the aisle, I chuckled inside remembering the time I'd been guest preaching at Zion prior to his marriage and had playfully asked, "Will the future Mrs.

Blade take a stand." Ten different women stood up! Of course, his future wife didn't stand because she knew where she stood. Dr. Blade was tremendous in both personality and his preaching. When we were together people often mistook one for the other; we were both dark-skinned, slim men. I once joked that when Mount Canaan called me, they really thought they were voting for Dr. Brady Blade, but were too polite to correct the error upon my arrival.

Jones, Blade, and I had an unofficial division of labor. Jones was in the area of politics while Blade was entrepreneurial; it seemed everything he touched turned to gold. My specialty was to assist the less fortunate. People must have quickly caught on to our divisions of duties; whenever they had a problem, they seemed to know which of us to consult.

As it turned out, dealing with the intricacies of white people and various situations as an activist was good preparation for dealing with my beloved brothers in the ministry. At one time or another, I had been appointed a leader at every level of my denomination, despite never pursuing those roles. In fact, I filled every position not because people desperately wanted me, but because they wanted to stop someone else from getting it. Apparently, I was always a good compromise.

My first experience with this dynamic came about in 1968, when I was elected president of the Baptist Ministers Fellowship in the Shreveport area. When the esteemed Dr. J. R. Retledge died, another minister was chosen to serve during the remainder of his term; however, the interim president's style was so different from his predecessor that the body did not want to elect him to a full term. They chose me instead.

A while later under similar circumstances, I became the moderator of the 13th District Missionary Baptist Association which consisted of churches and pastors. Dr. John B. Simmons was the moderator at the time and had served for many years. As he neared old-age, some of the other ministers thought it was time for a new leader to be appointed. Simmons suspected that a faction was trying to force him out, so he took a pre-emptive strike, telling the group, "You don't have sense enough to get rid of me. I'll step down when I'm good and ready; however, if my boy Harry would accept the position, I'll step down this year."

Well, that was all the group needed to hear. I knew they did not really want me, nor did I want the responsibility, so when they brought my name forth in a motion, I expressed to them that I was not interested. I was then asked if there was "unreadiness" (i.e. any hesitance or reservation on my part).

I answered honestly. "Yes, I have unreadiness. I don't want to be the moderator. I don't know how to be a moderator."

I went on to explain that I had committed to preaching 20 revivals a year and so would often be absent from the association's meetings and events. My concerns flew over their heads. All it took was for someone to say "All in favor, say aye," and they voted me in.

A similar matter resulted in my being chosen to lead the Louisiana State Baptist Convention. My predecessor, Dr. Theodore Judson Jemison, had been elected president of the NBC USA, Inc, and he caught wind of the consensus that he should not head both. Dr. Jemison called me to ask if, as his vice president,

I would go to the upcoming meeting. This was no run-of-the-mill meeting; the intention was to unseat him. It did not come easy, but eventually he agreed to resign. His resignation came with one condition: I had to be his replacement.

Again, I had no desire to be president. Since I did not have Dr. Jemison's credentials, I feared that my election might diminish the position or the convention. Upon hearing my objections, he told the rest of his cabinet behind my back, "Y'all better draft Harry Blake to be my successor because if you don't and then so and so gets elected, you will have no positions because he will kick all of you out because you are my supporters." When they thought about that, they promptly agreed. A campaign was put together, and I got elected.

My tenure was spent on efficiencies, consolidating the educational congress with the parent body and proposing a new schedule. The Louisiana Missionary State Baptist Convention became a model for state conventions across the nation. Today, it still is.

FAMILY LIFE

There were times when community obligations clashed with family obligations. Managing a church and fellowshipping with other churches meant that I was not spending as much time at home as was ideal. It devastates me to recall what a sloppy parent and husband I was. To cope with my disappointment in myself, I've had to erase failures from my memory. The only thing I recall with total clarity is how Norma made it all work.

We married in August of 1958. I had another year of college to complete so we only saw each other on weekends. She still lived with her parents, so on weekends I joined her at her parents' home. After I graduated, for a few months we shared a room in the Hollywood neighborhood with a long-time family friends, Mr. and Mrs. Stephens.

After a few months working at the bakery, we were able to save enough to move into a three-room shotgun house with Norma's sister Christell and her husband Melvan in Canaan Land, which was located between Lakeside and Queensborough before it was destroyed by the interstate. The only thing that survived I-20, was

Midway Number 1 Baptist Church (Midway Number 2 was displaced and had to move to Allendale).

In early 1961 a friend called Norma and I to tell us about a nice house for sale near them, 2834 Abbie Street where an elderly woman had died. Her daughter sold us the house, but it was really practically a gift. We paid only four or five thousand dollars for it. We remodeled it completely, adding two additional bedrooms and exterior bricks. We needed the extra space because our family was growing quickly.

Our first child, Mamie Elizabeth, had been born on December 26, 1959. While Norma was pregnant, my grandmother whose name was Mamie, said to her with an evidently suggestive undertone, "If someone comes to your house without a name, I think Mamie is a beautiful name." The inspiration behind Elizabeth, of course, was the first church I pastored. Norma had the lovely idea of combining the two names.

There is nothing like the experience of having your first child! It was such a joyous and wonderful time. Norma's family is much larger than mine, so all of her family was there as was my dad. Black people are so incredible. One of the most amazing things about us is our ability to experience elation even as racism pervades. Elizabeth was born at Confederate Memorial Hospital, so the reminders of oppression are even in the place's name. It was one of only two hospitals that admitted black people, but really it was two hospitals in one. Black patients were kept in a separate building that was dilapidated. Norma's care was subpar and black patients were not cared for by registered nurses. In lieu of a hospital bill, there was a requirement that a family member of the patient donate blood. Blood was, like everything else, segregated. In spite of all this, we felt blessed beyond measure.

When our next child was born in September 1961, Norma named him after me. I had never really liked the name Harry, but I fell in love with it when I considered the high honor my wife bestowed on me by naming our son after me. Norma continued her uncanny streak of giving birth after holidays, the first two having been born on days following Christmas and Labor Day. Our third child, Rodney, was born the day after Thanksgiving and several years later in 1968 our baby girl, Monica was born the day after Norma's birthday.

I love my children but over the years have restrained from publicly praising them, but this I must say; they were the best behaved boys and girls in the church. They didn't walk, talk or chew gum in church. You didn't have to give them candy or cookies or anything. The older women in the church would assist Norma with the young children. I was harder on our children than I was on other children, but there were certain families that spoiled our children. At a certain point I just felt they were receiving too many things and had to ask one of our dear friends, Ms. Ruby Babers to stop spoiling them.

As they became teenagers, they found their own roles in the church. Liz, Rodney, and Monica led songs. Norma had a lovely voice as well. In her younger years as a wife she sang in the choir and led songs. I didn't show it, but internally, it really warmed me.

If you had to compare Norma and me as speakers, Norma was a much better speaker. Norma could just get up and say a few words of welcome and people would shout all over church, so I never let her get up before I preached. The church used her often as a speaker, especially for Women's Day. She was very powerful. Norma was appreciative of how all of our churches treated us like family. They really doted on the children, treating them as if they were their own. Even our children saw our church as their second home, and the people in it as their family members.

After Norma stopped usurping our holidays with childbirth, church services were the focal point of such celebrations, especially Easter, which was an all day celebration that began at 5:30 a.m. with Sunrise Service. Mother's Day was always a packed service requiring overflow locations. Typically, my mother would join us at church then we would visit with Norma's mother in early evening. I always made sure Norma was treated like the queen she was. The children, especially the boys, knew I was adamant they never forget to honor their mother on all appropriate occasions. Norma liked money, so her purse would be weighed down with cards and cash. For most other holidays, church members would either invite us over to their homes or cook for us. I graciously accepted cakes from everyone but only ate my favorite, coconut.

While the children were young, Norma didn't work outside the home. I'd wanted her to continue to be a homemaker, but eventually, she began a career at Western Electric, which eventually became AT&T and closed under the Avaya name. During the summers while Norma was at work, I was responsible for the children, who would travel with me a great bit. One year I took Liz to one of the Baptist conventions. I didn't know how to do her hair, so some of the church ladies handled that duty for me. I taught the kids to drive on road trips to places like New York and

Atlanta. They got so good at driving that I felt comfortable napping in back. On one such occasion, I woke up to find Harry had driven over a hundred miles in the wrong direction. Of course, this was a time before GPS.

I performed the marriage of each of my children, except for Rodney's first marriage. He was so impatient he went to a justice of the peace. After our children grew up and left home, our home remained filled with games and laughter thanks to our grandchildren. Indeed, the last few years were our only ones without children around.

Now that Norma is no longer with me physically, and I have retired from Mount Canaan, life is even more different still. But change is good, and I look forward to what God has remaining for me to do and forever grateful for the lessons he's taught me thus far.

PHOTOS

I'm walking along the railroad tracks at Dixie Junction.
(Photo from Blake Family Photo Archives)

My parents' home in Dixie. *(Photo from Blake Family Photo Archives)*

The Whitlow General Store where I worked as a teenager.
(Photo from Blake Family Photo Archives)

The yards around tenant houses. *(Photo from Blake Family Photo Archives)*

The Big House on Woodspur Plantation.
(Photo from Blake Family Photo Archives)

The local commissary.
(Photo from Blake Family Photo Archives)

ME THROUGH THE YEARS
(Photos from Blake Family Photo Archives)

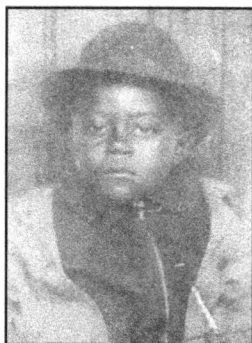

1937

ca. 1947

1949

1956

Graduation Photos

1953
Booker T. Washington High
School, Shreveport, Louisiana

1960
Bishop College
Dallas, Texas

Our family Christmas photo from 1961: Norma, Liz, Chubby, and Harry.
(Photo from Blake Family Photo Archives)

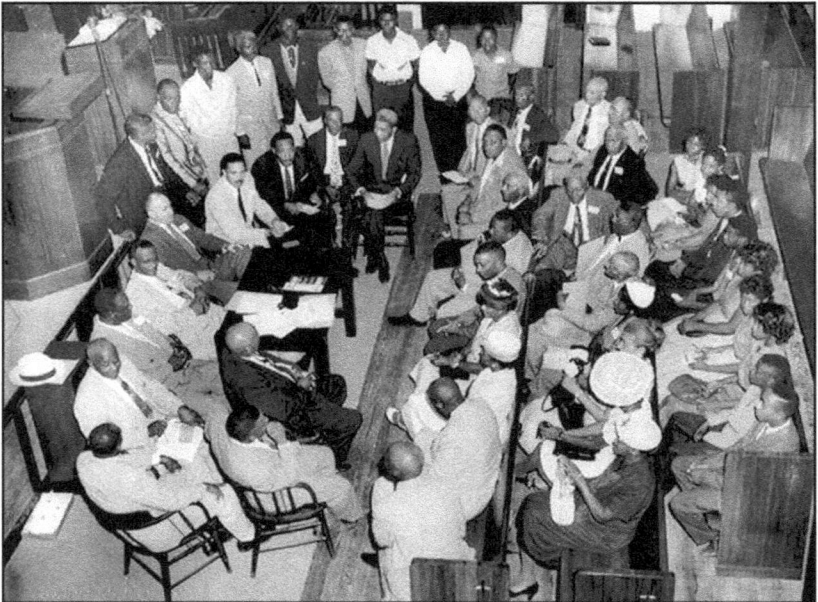

Local leaders meeting with Dr. Martin Luther King Jr. at Galilee Baptist
Church in Shreveport on August 14, 1958.
(Photo: Courtesy of Simpkins & Brock, LLC)

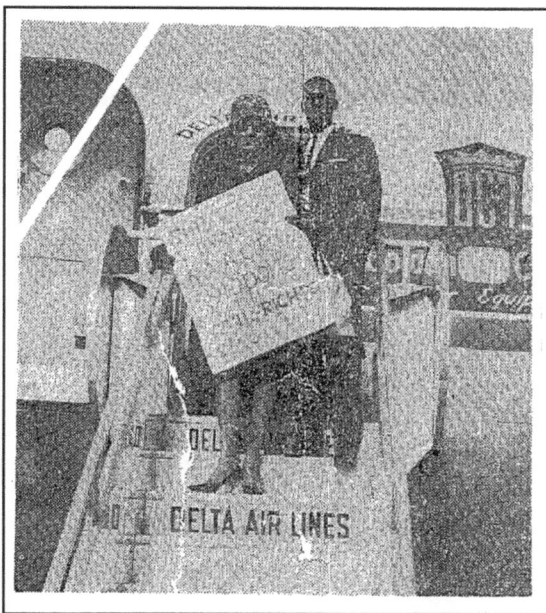

The Shreveport Sun captures photo of me and Ann Brewster as we board
an airplane to depart for the March on Washington in the nation's capital.
(Photo from Southern University Shreveport Archives)

The Shreveport Sun publishes photo of the bullet hole left in my car
following an assassination attempt.
(Photo from Southern University Shreveport Archives)

Over a thousand young people gathered at Little Union Baptist Church in Shreveport, Louisiana to hold a memorial service for the girls who had been killed in a bombing at the 16th Street Baptist Church in Birmingham, Alabama.

Photos on this page and the opposite page are provided courtesy of the Department of Archives and Special Collections, Noel Memorial Library, LSU Shreveport.

Police Halt March

Local Officers Use Riot Guns, Billy Sticks, Tear Gas

Sun

20 Students Injured At BTW Hi School

bodily to a paddy wagon after she reportedly appealed to policemen to "leave the campus and let teachers take care of

Local Citizens To Pay Tribute To Birmingham Six

Trustee Of Bombed Church Speaker

More than 2,000 Negro citizens of Shreveport are expected to participate in 'Memorial March' Sunday, Sept. 22, at 5 p. m. in memory of the six youngsters killed in Birmingham, Ala. last Sunday. Memorial services will follow at the Little Union B. C.

August 1963, Shreveport Sun headlines announcing the community's planned memorial for the children killed in the Birmingham Bombings and reporting the beatings citizens endured following the service. *(Photo credit Southern University Shreveport Archives)*

Police forcing me to show my ID before entering Little Union Baptist Church
(Photo credit: Langston McEachern)

Shreveport Commissioner of Public Safety George D'Artois watches as police officers taunt citizens at Little Union Baptist Church. As president of the local chapter of the NAACP, I'd helped organize the gathering at Little Union Baptist. *(Photo from the Southern University-Shreveport Archive)*

Police marching down Milam Street in front of Little Union Baptist Church.
(Photo from the Southern University-Shreveport Archive)

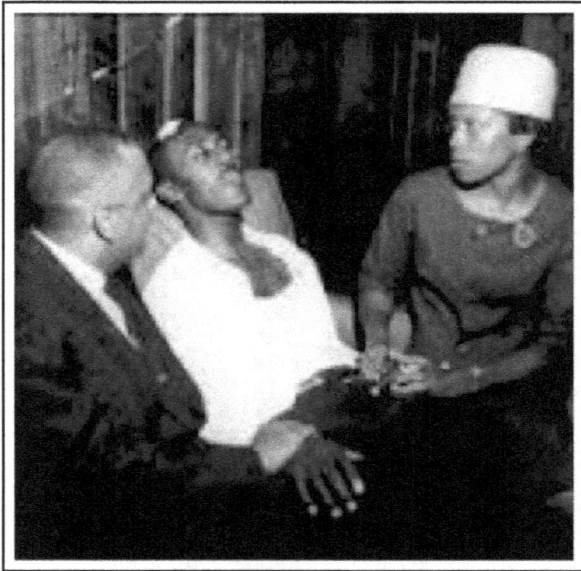

Norma comforting me following my beating by police.
(Photo from Blake Family Photo Archives)

Police beating students

Police marching to Little Union Baptist Church

Police with rifles standing over students.

Pictured here with Reverend Al Sharpton reviewing a plaque
commemorating the 40th Anniversary of police attacking me
and others at Little Union Baptist Church. Black citizens had come
together to hold a memorial to honor the four girls killed in the
16th Street Baptist Church bombing in Birmingham, Alabama in 1963.
(Photo credit: Michael Reagan. Blake Family Photo Archives)

With deacons of Mount Canaan Baptist Church in 1967.
(Blake Family Photo Archives)

With my deacons and deaconess at Mount Canaan in 1966.
(Photo from Blake Family Photo Archives)

Norma and I with our children, Rodney, Harry Jr. (Chubby), Elizabeth (Liz), and Monica in 1976 preparing for the dedication of the new sanctuary.
(Photo credit: Blake Family Photo Archives)

Norma and I with Senior Deacons at Mount Canaan in 1995.
(Photo from Blake Family Photo Archives)

At the National Baptist Convention USA, Incorporated.
(Photo credit: Denise Mayhan, photographer for NBCUSA, Inc.)

My photoshoot with Norma in 2016 *(Photo credit: Brittany Figaro. From Blake Family Photo Archives)*

Having a laugh with my wife, Norma, during a photoshoot in 2016.
(Photo credit Brittany Figaro. From Blake Family Photo Archives)

Another photoshoot with my beloved wife, Norma, in 2016
(Photo credit: Brittany Figaro. From Blake Family Photo Archives)

The Washington March *(Photo Credit: National Archives)*

PART 2

LETTER TO
ACTIVISTS

My fellow comrades,

You've chosen what is undoubtedly one of the most difficult professional paths. There is little glory or feeling of accomplishment and seldom is money in it. However, you substantially increase your chances of being injured or killed. Yet, there is something profound, peaceful, and fulfilling about fighting for what is right.

I knew something was wrong in America, and there started a burning inside of me and a yearning to analyze what I could do to alter the same. All I wanted was for America to treat black people the way it treated white people. For that, I was vilified. They said, "Harry Blake is a communist. He needs to wait."

It is the exact same thing they say to you today when you demand justice, so be encouraged, as you walk in the footsteps of Dr. Martin Luther King, Jr. and others like Muhammad Ali, who, though now praised, were demonized in their time.

Know that you are still needed on the battlefield. Modernity has merely brought innovative ways to oppress. They used to lynch us with rope. Now, though rope is still sometimes employed, more often, they use policies.

Yours for the cause of peace and equity.

LESSONS

FIGURE OUT HOW YOU ARE GOING TO EAT

S o many activists end up compromised or financially destitute. It is essential that you determine early on how you are going to make money since financial independence is of great importance. Nevertheless, this doesn't suggest that money is the most important thing. I hated every job I've ever had that made money. Jesse Jackson gave me a position. I was making forty thousand dollars, and I hated every second of it. I lasted six months.

During the time I worked for Dr. King, I made very little money. The two churches I led and the places where I preached also paid me. The work activists do is vital, but it doesn't change the fact that activists have to eat.

There is also the risk of being compromised. Having our own wealth is so important! It wasn't lost on me that the black folks who were most empowered during the Civil Rights Movement were the entrepreneurs: barbers, hairdressers, undertakers—they weren't relying on white folks for money.

I have a grandson, Jared, who has an entrepreneurial spirit. In high school, he would sell the kids candy and chips. Now he goes online and buys classic cars, restores them, and may make twenty thousand dollars profit by selling them. He learned this model from my son-in-law, Collier Mickle, who raised him. Collier owns a funeral home in Shreveport, and if they do less than twenty funerals a week, he's weeping because it was a slow week. What's more important than making money is that entrepreneurs aren't as easily controlled.

My daddy was the first entrepreneur I knew. Daddy was always good with money. The trend was if you worked on a plantation, you never made enough to get out of debt. The white plantation owner would pull out the ledger and say, "You did well, but you didn't make it out of debt."

I don't remember a single year my dad didn't get out of debt. He managed his money and relied on multiple sources of income. Everything we ate, we grew. My dad raised and sold geese and hogs and made more from his livestock and garden than from working on the plantation. In 1948, after the war, Daddy bought a brand-new car and paid cash for it, fifteen hundred dollars, I think, which he had kept hidden in the mattress.

My daddy was displaced by the tractor and wages when the law required plantation owners to pay cotton pickers minimum wage, the owner opted for mechanization and let field hands like Daddy go.

Although, Daddy was nearly an old man, yet he figured out a way to survive and even prosper. He discovered two acres of land with a shack not as good as the tenant house he occupied on the plantation house. He bought it. His new home had no electricity, but it was his, and there was enough land to raise hogs and garden.

In addition, sometime around 1967, we discovered that the Department of Agriculture had a program that helped rural people buy homes. Daddy qualified for a three-bedroom house with an indoor toilet. Some years later, he began to draw Social Security benefits. Daddy died with a paid-for house and money in the bank. This was made possible by a forced change to policies, which were brought about by activism. This is why, it is so necessary that we remain able to sustain ourselves while we continue to fight.

FIND LITTLE WAYS TO BE SUBVERSIVE

Oppressed people are never fully liberated. There are sputters, setbacks, and so forth. Those fighting injustice seldom get a big payoff. One has got to figure out how to get a little relief where one can.

I vividly recall a favorite lesson Daddy taught me. My daddy, as I think about it, was gifted in that he knew how to work the system. He knew he had to pay homage to the white man. He'd call them "Cap'n" and "Boss" and other terms of deference and elevation. He knew these things softened egotistical white men, and Daddy used this tactic to get what he needed to survive.

For instance, one day he said to me, "You can call a white man a dog if you know how and get by with it, make him like it even." He then showed me how.

Daddy walked over to the plantation boss, who was standing, admiring his new car. Daddy walked by the car and said, "Cap'n, this is a beautiful car. You know you're a big dog!" The boss smiled his biggest smiled and puffed out his chest a little, not realizing what Daddy had done. Daddy called the boss a dog and made him like it. Daddy mocked him to his face saying, "You know you're a big dog, ha ha ha!"

I saw my daddy using this technique to get what he needed without diminishing his manhood. No one ever controlled his mind.

Since, I had witnessed the power in this and started trying it out for myself. One time, this old white farmer came to Whitlow's store, needing to use the post office inside. I was out, sweeping the stoop of the store, and the man, trying to save himself a walk to the door in the event Whitlow had already closed the store and post office to take his lunch break, said to me, "Hey, boy! Is the post office open?"

Now, I was a boy by age, but I was not the kind of boy he called me. I'll also note that I was not HIS boy. Whitlow could call me "boy" because he signed my check. The white man who was yelling at me did not intend to pay me, so I refrained to answer him.

Shortly, the man came over to me, touched my shoulder, and said, "Hey boy, is the post office open?"

I continued my silent protest.

He went inside the store and said loud enough for me to hear, "Whitlow, where did you find that damn deaf and dumb nigger?" I laughed at that. He was so dumb he didn't know that I wasn't deaf.

My daddy taught me how to be a man, and a proud one, even during segregation and on the plantation. You have to do what is inevitable for your survival.

WHITE PEOPLE ARE LIKE ALL PEOPLE. THEY CAN BE EVIL. THEY CAN BE GOOD OR, AT LEAST, GOOD ENOUGH.

When I became the pastor of Mount Canaan, I went to see the mayor of Shreveport, Clyde F. Fant Sr. I wanted his support, but not at all cost. So I told him that I was the same Harry Blake who had protested and made a lot of noise and caused upheaval, and whenever deemed necessary, I wouldn't hesitate to do it again.

The mayor responded by asking, "Reverend, did you ever notice that each time you got arrested, you went before Judge Whitmire? That didn't happen by chance."

Although, as a person, Mayor Fant was nearly as nice a man as Mr. Whitlow, but Fant was a politician, and in that role, he knew how to satisfy white people, his voters. He found ways to help black people around the edges, but he didn't push white people because he knew, it would be a career suicide.

I had influence on elected officials. I would tell them, "I need housing. I want you to help me find funding."

Since, we were in a desperate need to build housing, we used an abandoned park that sat on about eight acres. I asked the mayor to give it to me. He got the city council to pass an ordinance, which suggested that the city's properties shall be used for religious, recreational, educational, and housing purposes only. As a result, the mayor persuaded them to sell the park to Mount Canaan. That's how we were able to procure the property to build the 120 multi-family complex.

Judge Whitmire was also somewhat good, but he was voted in too, so he had to appease white people. He never deviated from the status quo, but he tried to do what he could within his purview. Whenever I got arrested, Judge Whitmire would suspend my sentence, so I never stayed in jail.

As a whole, my relationship with whites was quite pleasant. When I graduated from high school, all those white people who patronized the Whitlow store gave me gifts. I ended up with more gifts from white people than from black people. Of course, this was because whites had more money to give me gifts.

Another example of my interaction with whites relates to the fact that for many years, I had a free loaner car from a local, white-owned car dealership. I knew the owner could do it because he was doing it for the Catholic Church a mile away, so I put him in the position to do it, and he did.

This was so, as I had a clear understanding that white people are as capable of kindness and fairness as black people, but they need the freedom, and sometimes historical context and education, to do it.

Dr. King and the Movement freed white folks as much as he freed blacks. This was on purpose. Dr. King wanted whites to be able to do what was right. There were a lot of white folks who wanted to do right, but they would be ostracized and even terrorized. Many white people lost their lives during the Civil Rights Movement, just as black activists did.

However, things were not always the same for us. George D'Artois, the public safety commissioner was an elected official, so the mayor could neither hire nor fire him. He had his own freedom and reported to no one. D'Artois was a tyrant and thought capable of doing anything. In 1964, when Ann Brewster, a beauty salon owner who had served alongside me at our local NAACP chapter, was found dead from a gunshot wound, no one in the black community believed the police report that determined she had committed suicide with a .38.

Just as he was known for being ruthless towards local black civil rights activists, he had earned a reputation for maintaining a similar behavior toward white people. It was widely believed that D'Artois had planned the murder of a white reporter named Jim Leslie. He was killed by a hired hitman shortly after reporting campaign irregularities. There were reports that people had heard D'Artois threatening to kill Leslie, but no one said or did anything to protect their fellow white man, who was only following the law and doing what was right.

D'Artois was in prison, awaiting his murder trial, when he died from a heart procedure. So there was no justice for the white Leslie, just as there was no justice for all the black people.

After we had achieved the height of the Civil Rights Movement, there was a robust effort to run me out of town as they had done with the father of the Civil Rights Movement, Dr. Simpkins. What they did to me was persuaded the mortgage company to cancel the insurance on my house and car, which meant the bank wouldn't finance the mortgage. A local businessman Mr. Hartner called me and said, "Preacher, I understand the problem you're having. Your house is not finished and the bank is foreclosing on you. How much do you need? I will lend you the money interest free for six months so that your house can be completed. While attending the NAACP conference in Chicago in 1963, my car was stolen; hence, my car payment became due. After I'd returned home, a car dealership owner in Chicago, who heard about what happened called me. The manager, Kim Novack, was employed at the Drexel Chevrolet Dealership in Chicago.

DON'T LET
THEM KILL
A SCARED
NIGGER

Death threats were an occupational hazard. When it came to humans, Miss Doll taught me to expect the worst but to endeavor to bring out the best in people. This country has a complicated racial history. This was especially true in places like "Bloody" Caddo Parish. The worst stories, those of assassinations, lynching, and burning crosses in front yards, I read about in the newspaper, but we experienced narrow escapes in our community as well. For instance, when St. Rest Baptist Church was bombed, most of us acted bravely. One of the fathers of Civil Rights and a local leader, Dr. C. O. Simpkins saw his house and office bombed, rendering him unable to continue his dental practice in Shreveport since his malpractice insurance was intentionally canceled. He was forced to relocate to New York.

The one threatening harm isn't always the boogeyman underneath a white sheet. I never knew anyone, or even of anyone, to be dragged from his or her home in the middle of the night by the local Ku Klux Klan. Every beating I had ever endured or witnessed was undertaken and executed by the police. Of course, we suspected many on the force were Klansmen, but it was something we were unable to prove.

Daddy was not a fearful man. I knew this because I'd witnessed him face the possibility of death. Daddy had learned to drive in the late 1930s. Back then, the roads were narrow and covered with gravel, so one driver had to give way when cars approached from the opposite direction, especially on a bridge. During one such encounter, Daddy accidentally swiped the car of a white man.

"Here he comes, Ike. Here he comes. Get out. Get out," Miss Doll said nervously.

The white man came over, and he began cussing. "Boy, you so and so, I ought to kill you."

Daddy calmly replied, "Well, I tell you what, Cap'ntain: I can't stop you from killing me, but you won't kill a scared nigger."

When we think and talk like that, white folks leave us alone. They say, "Oh, that nigger ain't got good sense." But what they knew was a person who isn't stifled by fear has real power.

Daddy modeled for me how to live fearlessly with the lurking possibility of death. When Daddy delivered to me a message from a white farmer in Dixie, who said that if he ever saw me in there, he'd kill me. I sent word back that he could find me driving through Dixie every Sunday morning between 9:00 and 9:30 a.m., on my way to the church I pastored, so he would have the opportunity to kill me once a week.

I got this courage from my Daddy. So, eventually when there was an assassination attempt on my life, I didn't shrink. It happened in 1960, at the beginning of my work with SCLC and Dr.

King. I was coming from a rural church, and as I was passing lanes, I heard the window crash. I thought someone had thrown a rock, but they had actually fired a gun. Had I not leaned forward at that very moment to adjust my radio, the bullet would have hit me. Instead, it lodged in the right passenger seat. I was mad, mostly because the impact of the glass had torn four holes in my new suit, and back then, I only had one.

I followed my impulse, which was not to flee but to follow the lone car that had pulled beside me just before the gun fired. I sped up to get the car's license plate. Of course, nothing came of my report to the sheriff, who said the owner of the car was bowling at the time of the incident, but they were on notice that I wasn't going away.

BE
DISCERNING

Daddy decided to spend the last decade of his life in a retirement home after living with me a few years following Momma's death. He liked care and constant company. He liked relaying to me conversations he had with other residents. On one such occasion, he recalled a story one gentleman had told him that concluded with the man asking, "Mr. Blake, you believe what I'm telling you, don't you?"

Daddy said he replied, "Yes. I believe anything told to me. I believe it is either the truth or a lie."

This could be the theme of any movement. The people who swore to protect all area residents were trying to sow seeds of dissension. They were trying to put a rift between Dr. Jones and me. They would call me to the police station and insinuate Jones was spying on me. They'd say, "There's a pastor who presides over a church behind the jailhouse who tells me everything you are planning to do."

Well, who was that? That was Dr. E. Edward Jones, my closest friend. The chief of police would tell me that to make me suspicious of my closest friend and employed the same tactic—make the accusations about me to Jones—to make him suspicious of me.

The two of us could have become paranoid because we used to have midnight planning meetings in Dr. Simpkins's office, and before daylight, the white man would, in fact, know what was said at the meeting! Logic would tell you someone at the meeting was a spy, but fifty years later, a report that became public revealed the truth: A recorder had been planted in the building by either the utility company or an electrician with access to the building.

Meaning I didn't fall for the white man's plot to convince me to distrust my brother. Having grown up on the plantation, I knew that tactic. Nevertheless, THEY did not have our level of insight about what was going on.

Often, things are not as they appear or are counterintuitive. It's like the heavy overalls and loose-fitting, long sleeve shirts we used to wear when picking cotton. At first glance, one would assume those clothes would be too hot under an already scorching sun, but in fact, the flapping clothes would retain the moisture from our perspiration, creating a cooling effect, especially when there was a breeze.

I knew Dr. Jones, and I knew I could trust him. He carried some of my secrets to his grave, and I'll take his secrets to mine. Being in possession of this knowledge is indispensable. It is the only way to maintain one's sanity, the only way to stay cool.

THIS WORK IS LONELY, ISOLATING, AND DISAPPOINTING

Though I knew I could trust Jones, there were black people I knew I couldn't trust. My parents trained me on human nature. People will disappoint you. People will lie to you and lie to your face. They will try to convince you that you said something you didn't say. They will try to betray you. They won't support the movement as you do. That's a right you can't take from a person. Only a few people will be committed at your level.

The knowledge that we couldn't count on law enforcement to enforce the law or to protect us was a terror in its own form. It led some black people to become cowards and, in some cases, traitors.

Shreveport was a vicious town, so terror was instilled and running rampant. One hears many of the folks saying, "Yeah, I was a part of the Movement," or "I was at Little Union when you got beat." No, they weren't. They weren't there. Claiming that has become popular, but one can't disprove that they weren't involved. So people come up to me and say, "Oh, I was with you," and I know they weren't.

Dr. King could not speak in any church in Shreveport. There were just a few black churches, which opened their doors to allow him to speak. I remember Dr. Simpkins's disappointment when the church trustee board on which he sat voted against allowing Dr. King to speak there for fear that the church would be bombed.

If I was walking downtown, I would see someone I knew walking towards me, and they would cross the street because they did not want to be identified with me publicly. I understood this and isolated myself to keep people out of harm's way. For instance, I loved my fraternity, but I couldn't risk going to Omega Psi Phi chapter meetings with my buddies because many of them were teachers or worked for the city. I didn't want to make them uncomfortable, or worse, as their association with me could lead to their being ostracized at work or even fired.

Talking about the traitors, it was quite difficult to understand the black people who spied on us and reported back to the police. Everybody knew one particular informant. He wasn't an officer, but he worked for the police department. Some saw him as a traitor but he saw himself as a man making a living, bettering himself. He chose personal gain at the expense of advancement for all his people. Eventually, I was able to forgive him, but I wonder if he was ever able to forgive himself.

PRACTICE
FORGIVENESS

The Bible says more about how to treat an enemy than it does about how to treat a friend. I suppose God assumed we would know how to treat our friends.

What does the Bible say? God instructs us to love our enemies, feed them if they're hungry, give them drink if they're thirsty, do good to those who hate us, pray for those who abuse us. Why?

I suppose this is God's way of being subversive because these tactics are deadly. I have tried them and found kindness is a sure way to kill. Either the enemy's hate will die, or the enemy will commit psychological suicide, self-sabotage.

Hence, to carry out God's instructions, I had to forgive first. This was difficult. At the end of my tenure as a career activist, I was angry with so many people. I was angry with the people who had prioritized their financial livelihood over lifting the race. I was angry with the black people who had profited from their betrayals. I was deeply hurt by the black and white leaders, who watched me being assaulted but wouldn't lift a pen to publicly denounce what had been done to me. Eventually, I came to myself and recognized I was wrong to condemn people for not having my level of commitment. They hadn't asked me to commit my life to this, so they owed me nothing. Nobody called a meeting or said, "Rev. Blake, we want you to be our leader." The community didn't vote me to be the leader of the Civil Rights Movement. Instead, I chose it, so no matter what happened to me, I could not blame people for not embracing me. Therefore, I forgive the blacks who did not come to my defense.

There's a scripture in the Bible that can be paraphrased as follows: While God's friends slept, an enemy came and sowed seeds. There wasn't much difference between the white man—my working enemy—and my sleeping black friend. Since I forgave the one, I had to forgive the other, though it took much longer. I then watched God work.

George D'Artois was one of the true villains of the Civil Rights era. He was right up there with George Wallace and Ross Barnett, the white supremacist and separatist governors of Alabama and Mississippi. But when I decided to become the head of a church, I knew that, for the sake of my congregants, I had to make peace with this evil man. I needed his assistance to help the members of my church. I went to him as I had gone to the mayor and recited the same refrains and urged him not to try me because the things I'd done once in the Movement, I'd do again if need be.

D'Artois was also willing to be more amiable to me compared to another activist, Larry "Boogaloo" Cooper, whose rhetoric sounded more militant. While I was associated with the buttoned-up Christian, non-violent form of protest, Boogaloo's rhetoric was more militant and bombastic, making him appear capable of violence. The white establishment much preferred to deal with me. I refused to undermine Boogaloo, but I understood the dynamic.

Over the years, D'Artois and I managed to build a working relationship. Once, I even invited him to Mount Canaan during one of his reelection campaigns. The people couldn't believe I allowed D'Artois in my sanctuary and given what they perceived to be an endorsement. They wondered what that man could be holding over me. He wasn't holding anything over me; he was just the lesser of the evils.

As I've said, white terrorists don't inflict their violence only on black people, and D'Artois was no exception in this regard. Just as he was rumored to have murdered a prominent black woman and allowed the segregationists in the White Citizens Council to have their way in the black community. Apart from this, he had also allowed corruption to permeate all of Shreveport for a decade or so. The New Orleans crime boss was his friend. He ruled with an iron fist until the walls started to cave in on him. In the late seventies, he was charged with felony theft, intimidation of grand jury witnesses, and jury tampering during the trial related to the assassination of Jim Leslie, a former journalist he'd hired to manage his campaign.

When he knew the police were coming to arrest him, he became suicidal and hid in his attic. At his lowest point in life, he called me and asked me to pray for him. Without hesitation, I did.

THE STRUGGLE WILL BE WITH YOU ALWAYS. EMBRACE IT, AND DON'T FORGET HOW TO BE HAPPY.

For a long time, black people have been oppressed the world over. This is especially true in the United States, where, whenever we learn the America's game, they change the rules. Whether one is a formal activist or merely exercising one's rights, the struggle never ends, nor should it.

I remember, years after having given up my professional role in the Movement—it was maybe as late as 1967—I went to a live-stock auction to sell some hogs for my daddy. Jim Crow was no longer the law of the land, but folks were still segregating themselves. I sat on the side with the white folks. A white farmer I knew from Dixie came over and said, "Harry, we're not ready for this. You need to sit on the other side."

I stayed put. This was the moment I realized two things, that some people are never going to do what is right if they aren't forced to and that if one is on the side of right, there is no leaving the Movement because the cause is in that person. This is the struggle of a lifetime. This isn't daunting to me because I also realize there is strength in the struggle.

Often, I fondly tell young people the story of the little boy who grew tired of waiting for a butterfly to emerge from its cocoon. One day, the boy saw the thing inside was struggling to get out, so he took a penknife and cut the butterfly out. The boy found, however, that the butterfly was unable to fly. It turns out that struggling to get out of the cocoon was strengthening his wings. Without that struggle, the wings couldn't fly. The same is true for us. It is my opinion that we have produced a generation who have wings but can't fly. In our effort to protect our children from struggle, we have produced a generation who can't fly.

This also denies one moment of great pride. Sure, there have been times when I wondered whether the sacrifices my family and I made were worth it. Then I remember my sister Carol telling me about the care and pride my parents always took in getting dressed up to go to the polls to vote. Although Daddy couldn't read, there was someone who could help him vote. They knew that their boy Harry played a role in that. That meant the world to me.

I also learned from my mother how it is possible to find joy and whimsy in life, no matter how hard it is. She loved to laugh and play with her children. She would sing to me and tell me stories about the "Little Boy on the Wagon." Amazingly, it wasn't until I was an adult that I realized the stories were about me.

LETTER TO PARISHIONERS

My dearest Mount Canaan,

When I came in 1966, you wanted me and showed me love in a very real way; however, I wanted to follow my heart in many ways and not the way the Lord was leading. See, to come was to take a cut in pay, yet not to come was to go my own way—not completely trusting God.

After fifty-two years, I can honestly say it's been a good journey. I have met and cared for your families, and they have become members of my own family. My children found here everything they needed—mentors, grandparents, playmates, prayer partners, and lifelong friends.

During my many travels, you were the ones who were there for my wife and children to ensure their safety. Not only did you keep them safe, but you provided genuine love.

As I leave this place, behold that you will always be in my heart and that I wish only the best for you and your new pastor. I believe you have found the one, God had already chosen for you and we both know God does all things well.

Love and care for him and his family, love one another as Christ has also loved you, and be forgiving and long-suffering, as God commands. Most importantly, I urge you to trust God. Know that He knows what is best, and He will provide all that you need. Much of it has already been provided.

May the spirit of grace and generosity continue to abide in you.

LESSONS

BE ORDERLY,
WHICH
STARTS WITH
TIMELINESS

Everyone in the church, from the pastor to the pew member, has a role to play in maintaining orderly worship service. This task falls heavily on leadership—the preacher, deacons, and musicians—who have the authority to lead the service. I know some churches embrace spontaneity during service, say, an impromptu testimony or hymn; however, Paul instructed us that "all things should be done decently and in order."

By being orderly and intentional and thoroughly planning the elements within a service so that they flow "one by one," and the pastor leads the congregation into a deliberate focus on worshiping the Lord and allow the ENTIRE congregation to participate.

God gives every person the same amount of time—the same number of minutes and seconds. It's what each person does with it that matters. I grew up in the era of all-day services in the Baptist tradition. We didn't have TVs, video games, and all this stuff to distract us, as we do now. The Church was our social life.

I think I know where this comes from. During slavery, good slave masters would allow slaves to go to church on Sundays, but they were required to go back to the field after church. Well, if they stayed at the church until after sundown, they couldn't go to the field.

However, now is the time that we break this habit. It doesn't take all day to worship God. As a matter of fact, when the church is out, I don't want to listen to any more sermons or even gospel music. I want to do something else—be a good husband, father, or friend.

In addition, I'm not a preacher people shout on. I don't give them a show. I remember that after my very first sermon, all the old ladies came to me, saying, "That was such a good speech." "We really enjoyed your speech." Just recently, a lady came up to me after church and said, "Pastor, I really enjoyed your speech."

People run out of patience with me, so I keep my sermons short and to the point. Not everything is to be done in Sunday worship service. I inherited a church that was heavy on testimony and long prayers.

I remember one sister who loved giving long testimonies. How was I going to get the mic away from her without being rude or mean? Then something said to me, "hug her," so I did and pretended to whisper in her ear but said into the mic, "You can't tell it all, can you?" She said, "No, pastor." I replied, "Well, don't try."

The congregation appreciated that I respected their time, and her family appreciated that I hadn't embarrassed her. It was a win-win. (Of course, the next time I tried this technique, on a visiting worshiper who was going on and on while impatient worshipers began to walk out, I "You can't tell it all, can you?" She replied, "No pastor, but I'm going to try.")

I was taught that the attention span is short.

We all, myself included, are sometimes guilty of trying to tell it all. Of course, I was always lucky to have my wonderful wife, Norma, who'd remind me after a lengthy sermon. "Harry, you can't preach everything in one sitting, so don't try." So when I get up to preach, I think about that.

Norma had me see that people would rather have you sit down prematurely and leave them wanting more than to drag on. Even if they don't walk out on you physically, they do so mentally. It is the job of the one preaching the sermon or speaking to ensure everyone stays engaged.

EMOTIONS CAN BE DESTRUCTIVE TO THE CHURCH

Everywhere I've pastored, I've had good, positive relationships with my members. In fact, Mount Canaan had a reputation for not being able to keep pastors. In its hundred twenty-four year history, its longest pastor's tenure before I arrived had been twelve years. I completed fifty-two years. I believe my temperament has had something to do with that.

For a reason to believe, I don't want to appear against black expression in church. I am emotional. I do weep, and I feel moved, but I try never to let my emotions control me. Growing up, I saw most people letting their emotions get out of control. My daddy was one of the few people in my life who didn't behave that way. He was quiet. Rather than reacting at the moment, he would think things through.

Evocative preaching has long been the standard in the black church. I grew up in an era and community where worship was driven by heightened emotion. Ministers yelled their sermons and were theatrical. They did this when they preached, when they sang, when they opened the doors of the church, and especially at funerals. The audience responded in kind. People screamed and hollered when they lost someone. Pastors would flame the fire—they'd holler, the family would fall apart, and ushers would have to carry them out.

Everyone, including me, gets excited by a rousing sermon. I just thought something was missing and something was wrong about that. Moreover, I realized early on in my career that I simply didn't have that gift, so in my sermonic presentations, I tried instead to get people to see what the Bible says. It has worked in my church.

I tease Mount Canaan now about how they used to fight, and I mean literally, balled fists swinging! They wouldn't fight me, mind you. In fact, they'd wait until I was away from the church to fight in the parking lot. I would go out of town and come back to news of a brawl. Finally, I had a church meeting and said, "Anyone who wants to fight, do it now."

Eventually, I was able to get the church to see that God gave us emotions for a reason. They become negative when we allow them to control us and we don't control them.

THE CHURCH
IS A GARDEN

Life is a mixture of good and bad, evil and good, strong and weak, so how does one handle life when it rains? Not every day is going to be a shiny day, so begin each day prepared to handle the storms. None of us can stop the rain, but some of us are better equipped to control how wet we get, while others may drown.

From this rain, grow both the wheat and weeds of which Matthew spoke. We can't pull out the weeds without damaging some of the harvest, so they must grow together. This is true of both the garden and the church.

The church is made up of Christians of varying maturity levels. Some are grown, while others are spiritual infants—believers who aren't strong in their faith or rooted in the teachings and authority of God's Word. They are more likely to sow seeds of anxiety, strife, jealousy, and other conflicts.

If the church isn't careful, the weeds can overtake God's garden, so mature Christians must continuously feast on the Word, the nourishment that gives them the ability to discern truth from error. As they grow closer to Christ through prayer and obedience to His Word, they gain a greater understanding of Scriptures and are able to withstand the storms that arise. They are able to make sound and Bible-based decisions in their personal lives and in church policy.

It is through this example that child-like Christians can experience continued spiritual growth and a transformation of the mind as they learn and obey Scripture.

REMEMBER,
YOU ARE THE
COMMUNITY'S
SANCTUARY

hen I first visited Mount Canaan, I told the people that our church could not just reside in the community and we had to devise a plan to get the community into Mount Canaan. The love that was on the inside of the church, had to permeate the whole community. It is hard to keep people away from a person when they know that person loves them. I spent two to three years making sure the community knew they were loved.

I walked the streets of Allendale, listening to the residents talk. One of the grave mistakes we make is thinking that we know what they need without taking the time to find out what they really need. I spent so much time listening to people and feeling their pain. I sought to gain their confidence by going where they were and sitting where they sat.

The people were not happy with their environment. It was a depressed community with unpaved streets, outdoor toilets, and poverty permeated the air.

They needed better housing and the children needed something positive to do. I invited the mayor to ride with me throughout the community so he could witness what the people in the community saw. The first thing we noticed were the children playing in the streets, since no recreational facility was available for them. I asked the mayor to provide a portable swimming pool with lifeguards for the summer months and set it up in the parking lot. The mayor did this to allow me to change the culture of the children in the community, to give them a place of their own.

The kids responded in kind. Prior to the pool installation, Mount Canaan had to replace a broken windowpane every week, but I can't recall a broken window in the last forty-eight years.

Norma worked with a nutrition program, which involved going into communities and designating a certain house where children and parents would gather and she taught them how to cook healthy meals. In subsequent years, we instituted a summer feeding program, which provided breakfast and lunch for children from low-income households.

Assisting the community never stops. It is also not to be measured by a number. We have provided housing to hundreds of families. Five years ago, we started a home study support program for the sole purpose of educating just one little boy.

After the young lad had joined our church, I realized he was doing terribly in school. He couldn't read. Honestly, I have to restrain my tears when I talk about him because I remember struggling in school myself. I also knew the prison industrial complex was preparing his jail cell. I wanted Mount Canaan to help this boy and became frustrated with our members, especially those with master's and doctorate degrees. I said to them, "Let's homeschool him."

Around this same time in 2013, Dorothy Thompson came into my office seeking my advice as she was preparing to retire. She'd been in the school system for thirty-four years and had actually been awarded Teacher of the Year! Boy did I know exactly what she should do next! I was so fortunate she agreed with my idea to start a home study support program at Mount Canaan. In addition to the boy who inspired the program, we identified a few more boys who participated in Mount Canaan's Canaan Boys Academy, summer enrichment program who we believed would benefit from the learning environment we intended to create. While starting a school is a protracted process, the parents only needed to sign a few documents to become custodians of their children's educations. They then turned the boys over to us.

We have largely kept to our early model whereby the boys attended class from 8:30 a.m. to 3:00 p.m. During the school day, we provide the boys with two free meals. They wear uniforms comprised of a tie, oxford shirt, slacks, and for special occasions, blazers. If need be, the boys can shower and do their laundry at the church. There is a barber who comes by weekly to cut their hair.

Instruction is provided by several teachers, as well as a teacher's aid and a board certified counselor. Under this tutelage, the boys have made great strides in the last five years. The boys were at different skill levels. One young man had behavior issues and was a non-reader who didn't even know the sight word list but was in fifth grade. But we discovered that when he was regularly given his meals and medication, he was a different kid. The one student who couldn't read, he is a student who has great social skills. Academically, he had not been presented with the tools he needed to be literate. Literacy was a problem in his home, so this year, he'll receive more one on one. He will enter a program called Youth Build, which is offered through Southern University, which provides trades He would learn a trade then he could also enter the HISET program to get his GED. He's working really hard to save money to take the driver's license exam.

Three of the students have advanced enough to begin virtual school. Three of them are going to 9th grade. Academically, they have exceeded our expectations.

We created such a nurturing and safe environment that these young men will stay at the church as long as they can. We are providing them with opportunities. Spirituality, socialization, learning, and teaching them to be the best they can be. They have been exposed to golf, tennis, and bowling,

Mount Canaan, along with a prominent white business owner, Mr. Ivan Smith, have underwritten experiences and travel that we hope will broadened their world view. These include trips to see historical and cultural attractions in cities that were significant during the Civil Rights, like Memphis, Birmingham, Selma and Atlanta, as well as places of cultural significance, including Philadelphia, Baltimore, New York, and Washington, D.C.

None of these young men live in homes with their fathers, so we have tried to give them positive male role models. There is a deacon who is on the church staff who is former military, Deacon Donald Hughes. He is a strict disciplinarian and they respond well to him. Additionally, attorneys, doctors, teachers, professional men, even NFL players, have spoken to our students. This work is as meaningful as any I have ever done.

POWER OF
PRAYER

Not one morning of my life did I wake up without hearing my momma pray. Black folks know prayer works because we had to pray our way through slavery, Jim Crow, mistreatment, injustice, and setbacks. The hope was in our ability to pray, and we saw God make ways for us.

The first church I grew up in, didn't have a mission society or vacation Bible school, but we always had a prayer meeting, a time when the church would gather to pray. A week of prayer even preceded the revival.

While personal prayer has its own place, corporate prayer is vital. There is power in believers gathering to call on the Holy Spirit. The process is edifying. It leads us to be more aware of the burdens of others. It is a place where we can lift the needs of fellow servants in Christ and be reminded of how much we need prayer. We must remember that the ability to communicate with God came at the highest price, Christ's blood, so the privilege of prayer meeting is greater than the inconvenience of it.

At a certain point, however, the church lost its passion for prayer. The altar call became a substitute for prayer meeting. For the first twelve years of my tenure at Mount Canaan, prayer meeting attendance was between zero and seventeen people. I believed this to be devastating for the church, so I sought to restore the spiritual pillar of prayer. I sought to lead the church to let God's house be the house of prayer since God said in scripture, my house should be called the house of prayer.

For twelve years, my pleadings fell on deaf ears even if I fussed and cussed. I'm not proud of this, but I must confess the thing that really convinced me. In fact, it was the revelation that the white mayor of Shreveport's son, who was my friend in the ministry and pastored a church in Belcher, Louisiana where I had pastored also, had fewer members but a greater turnout for prayer service, and he didn't even whoop when he preached!

So I challenged my church. I said, "I need you to help me figure out if God is prejudiced. I've been taught the white man's ice is colder, sugar sweeter, etcetera. I need to know if this is what explains why the white man has a bigger turnout to pray."

Of course, they could find nothing in the Bible to support white people inherently being better at praying (or anything else) than black people. Our church simply had to commit to coming together to pray.

At the suggestion of one of my deacons, we decided to study the book of Acts, specifically, we followed the twenty-eight chapters, which focus on prayer. In those chapters, the church was either praying, saying something about prayer, or having a prayer meeting. The most powerful revelation to many was that the disciples never sought to learn how to perform miracles or speak in tongues or preach. They wanted to learn to pray.

Convincing my deacons, and then the church body, of the significance of prayer was my most successful church endeavor.

God said he wanted his house filled so that was a challenge for me, but we went from our dreadfully low attendance to six hundred. Today we average several hundred. The plan we used to restructure the prayer meeting and train our members is now a model used throughout the country. We have moved the church to what Jesus intended when he said, "My house shall be a house of prayer."

THE CHURCH IS THE MOST POWERFUL CIVIL RIGHTS INSTITUTION

T he church has always been the heart of the community, since historically; it was the only public space where black people could assemble. The black pastor was free to preach social justice gospels. In this respect, he differed from his white counterpart who ministered to slave owners, white supremacists, and accomplices and was thus burdened with competing for economic interests. Additionally, to preach about equality was to preach against the law, since discrimination was legal at that time.

At a certain point, the Civil Rights Movement that included demonstrations, boycotts, and marches went out of fashion. No march in recent years has or can have the impact of the 1963 March on Washington because no group since has been as oppressed. Doors were shut in our faces. We couldn't go to Holiday Inn even if we had the money.

On the contrary, when we got the doors open, we realized we didn't have the money to pay for the Holiday Inn. What good is it to be able to enter an establishment if you can't patronize it?

This revelation led to the second phase of the Civil Rights Movement, black people having the ability to make and manage money. Therefore, I sought to advance the race through economic empowerment. I started building houses for the poor, establishing daycare centers for working parents, and building a network in the community whereby I could recommend black people for jobs.

During my time at Mount Canaan, we built two major developments. The first was a 120 unit multi-family complex, which cost over two million dollars to build, and of which not one black person made a dime. While I was happy to have the facility for our community, it troubled me that the architect, builders, and lawyers were all white. I thought this was insane, so for our second project, which was a four-million-dollar high-rise senior living facility, I sought to hire an all-black team. I had lined up a black contractor in Houston, a black architect from California, and a black attorney in Shreveport. Interestingly, while white government and business leaders had never had a problem with everything being white-owned and operated, key parties objected to my all-black slate. In the end, we had to compromise.

DON'T
FORGET TO
CARE FOR
AND FEED
YOURSELF

We are hard-pressed to read the Bible and not see Jesus focusing on physical needs. He fed the hungry. He gave sight to the blind. He healed the paralytics. Often, Jesus addressed physical needs before spiritual ones. An infirmed Christian cannot be all he or she needs to be spiritually. Likewise, the church is still about the people. People have social, spiritual, economic, educational needs. God is concerned about the whole man, so the church has to be concerned about the whole man. The man has a body that needs to be fed, clothed, and housed.

The church can't do real ministry if the congregants are bogged down with their own problems. What I tried to do at Mount Canaan was to help members in every area of their lives, including financially; they needed to have stability. I heard all of my life that in America, money talks and people who have no money have nothing to say. This seems to follow blacks in life, so I tried to teach Mount Canaan, how to make and save money.

I'm a saver. I acquired that skill from my Daddy who when he died, still had a dime for every dollar he ever made. He was a very frugal man who never made over twenty-five dollars a week, but never bought anything on credit and died with savings in the thousands. He did this as I do, by budgeting. I have separate accounts for everything—family savings, personal splurges, emergency funds, giveaways, and my tithes to the Lord. I decided as a youngster that I would rather have a hundred thousand dollars in savings and drive a used car than have a fancy car and no savings.

Whether people make a little or a lot, they seem to face difficulty managing money. Daddy always anticipated a rainy day. People don't do this enough. When disaster strikes, we are surprised. We live from paycheck to paycheck. We may be making $100,000 a year, but nothing is saved. We don't know what to do when the money stops.

Mental and physical fitness are just as important as one's finances. The body is the temple of the Lord, and the spirit can't function well in a sick body. Eat right and exercise. We think of suicide being the immediate taking of one's life, but many of us commit suicide when we sit at the table with a plate, knife, fork, and food in front of us.

Our mental health is also important. At a certain point, I realized I was spending more time counseling, for which I was never formally trained, than fulfilling any other task in the church. But what I discovered was that often we have members who are qualified and certified to take on these duties. In this instance, I discovered in our congregation that Deacon Andrew Wilson was a trained and certified counselor. I asked him to take over the counseling ministry and he happily agreed.

Prayer is power, but there are some problems and issues that can't be prayed away. One must take care of the spiritual side, as well as the physical and psychological ones, to lead a better life.

PUT FIRST THINGS FIRST—FAMILY

I never heard it preached, nor did it come to me until I was older, how significant the family was. God wants us to put the family in focus. If I don't put God at the center of my family, I may just be going through the motions.

God created the family before he did the church, and God wants us to focus on the family because the church is made up of families. If we don't get the family right, the church will be misguided.

The first miracle Jesus performed was not at church, but at a home wedding, turning water into wine.

Healthy marriages are extremely important. I became alarmed when Mount Canaan had a period during which divorce rates were out of control. It broke my heart. When I perform marriages that end in divorce, I feel the way I imagine surgeons feel when they lose a patient.

The Bible defines death with one word—separation. Therefore, divorce is the death of a marriage.

When this was happening at Mount Canaan, I tried to examine why because there can be many reasons for a marriage to break down. In Mount Canaan's case I realized that too often, I had inadvertently played a role at Mount Canaan. I called all the men together, and I said I wanted to help them restore and have good marriages. I felt partially responsible for the divorce and separation that was taking place in our church. God revealed to me that there were marriages in which the woman was more committed to the church than her husband. As pastors, we unknowingly require women to be at the church all week—on Tuesday for the teachers' meeting, Wednesday for the prayer meeting, one night for youth rehearsal—and then they got up on Sunday morning and left their husbands alone in bed. Women were in church all day because they traveled with their pastor to an afternoon service. Add to this work and household responsibilities, they were always tired or irritated and unresponsive to meeting their husbands emotional and nuptial needs.

I saw that over time, this was taking a toll and causing marriages to die, which was, in some ways, more painful than physical death. When one physically dies, we inter the body, but with a divorce, the body continues to walk around. Rather than have my members endure such pain, I tried to create a church that supported couples.

TAKE CARE OF YOUR PASTOR AND HIS FAMILY

Pastors have neglected the responsibility of teaching the congregation how to treat the pastor. Maybe because we're self-conscious, but since it is in the Bible, it ought to be taught. I have been one of those pastors who dared to touch what others shied away from.

In 1 Thessalonians chapter 12 and 1 Corinthians chapter 9, Paul defends his right to be supported by the church financially. *Which man goes to war at his own expense? Which soldier enlists in the military and gets a job to buy his uniform, his food, his healthcare?* The military provides those things, but as a pastor, I have to buy my own clothes and robes. If military personnel get sick, they can go to a military doctor, so the church should have insurance for the pastor. When military personnel retire, they have retirement. The military provides additional training and vacation. Far too many churches do not perceive these things as their responsibility, even though in the old testament economy, those provisions were provided to the Levites and the priests.

In this context, the Bible reveals Christians as being soldiers in a spiritual battle, and the pastor is on the front line. The church members are to pray for the pastor to lead and protect their souls and to teach them how to handle this warfare.

Furthermore, one of the biggest challenges of a pastor is showing members what a real, dedicated pastor must do. The Bible draws a clear distinction between a shepherd and a hired hand. The community sees the pastor perform for thirty minutes on Sunday, and that's it. It is quite hard for them to see how much time he has to spend in preparation. When we look at the apostles, who were the founders of the church, we come to know that their priority was the ministering of prayer and preaching. Preaching means more than the emotional side; it means studying the word that was written in a language, we don't even speak. To understand it, one must spend three to seven years studying the language formally and then a lifetime more.

In addition, the pastor is responsible for overseeing everything that goes on in the church. At Mount Canaan, there are at least thirty people on the sick and shut-in list every week. It is impossible to visit them all every week, and that is why the pastor has to equip people to be able to assist.

In fact, Pastors are more prone to becoming addicts and alcoholics than other professionals because they are constantly dealing with problems. It takes a toll on the pastors' marriage, children, and mental health.

The prophet, Elijah, had emotional problems. He wanted to die. He didn't really mean it because when he heard Jezebel's death threat, he fled for his life, but he was depressed. Moses also got depressed to the point where he wanted to die. Therefore, even the godliest men and women continue to have these issues.

When I started at Mount Canaan, I made five thousand less than I had at my two previous part-time churches combined. I had such a rocky start with Mount Canaan that I could not have imagined how good this place would be to my family and me.

At my second rural church, that was the first thing I dealt with when I went to accept. We spent, I guess, four hours discussing what the salary would be, and they said to me that their last pastor had been there for twenty-seven years and they were paying him, I think, $50 a Sunday. They wanted to have Sunday services and to pay what they'd paid him.

The deacons and I argued. Finally, I said "Let the church decide what my salary will be and I'll accept what the church decides." I wish all churches would be as generous and kind as mine have been to me.

LETTER TO
PASTORS

Brothers,

Only you understand this life I've lived. Only you know the internal struggles with pride, impatience, and insecurity, as well as the elation of winning souls to Christ.

In my youth, I enjoyed good preaching and looked up to pastors, but I don't believe there was a single pastor in the community I came from, that had even a high school degree. This limited the ways that I could learn from them, and so my mentors became the great men of faith I was introduced to in books. This is where I first met Dr. Benjamin Mays and Dr. Martin Luther King, Jr.

Finally, in college, I found you, my comrades in the ministry. Our campus Lyceum was designed for comradery amongst students in religious studies. We would talk about sermons we preached on the weekend. Not all of the guys got a chance to preach a lot. Some of us did share the topics of our sermons whenever and wherever we preached.

Being among you in such settings was such a blessing to me. Around you, I could relax and have fun, let my metaphorical hair down. You are some of the most hilarious folks I've ever met. You are also honest, kind, and dynamic.

Together, we have made it through some very difficult and trying times. No assembly has matched the fellowship I find with you. I have appreciated your holding me accountable. Your criticisms have made me a better pastor.

May we all continue to come together and live God's will.

LESSONS

REGARDING MY DEEP ADMIRATION AND LOVE OF CHRISTIAN WOMEN

Pastors have different ministries. One of my main ones is to lift up Christian men for church leadership. I spent my life developing men to be godly in their homes, communities, and churches. Because I believe the Bible calls men to be spiritual leaders in the church, I strove to equip men at Mount Canaan to embrace their God-given role and to benefit the church with their spiritual gifts; however we can't do anything without women.

I thank God for the service of women in the church. They have always played a pivotal role. As a child, I admired how regal the first ladies, choir members, and missionaries were. The only thing that surpasses their beauty is their brilliance. It is my opinion that women are far smarter than men. I figured this out in high school and made sure to always run a slate of women with me when I ran for class president. We always won! If I had a project I needed to be done to perfection, I would give it to a woman, and it was done perfectly. They are strong, loving, and spiritual. They always have my admiration, especially because, for as good as they are, they always support us, 'Men'. Every time we have a men's day, women fill up the church, supporting their men. They make us better in every way, which is why men must do all that we can to be great leaders.

DON'T
COMPETE.
COLLABORATE.

As I've mentioned, Dr. E. Edward Jones and Pastor Brady Blade have been my best friends in the ministry. We knew each other's secrets and strengths and supported each other, but we were not without our insecurities.

One thing I struggled with was having two friends who were great preachers because I didn't consider myself even a good one. Nobody shouted when I preached. There was a time when Blade, who's a few years younger than I am, needed nurses standing by. Paramedics were routinely called due to so many people being overcome with the Holy Spirit and shouting. Once, at a revival in Marshall, Texas, a man was so overcome with the Spirit that he ran through the wall.

As I found myself struggling with the knowledge that my preaching was inferior to theirs, the Lord asked me these questions:

Do they have good churches?

I replied, "Yes."

Do you fill churches?

I replied, "Yes."

Do you get invitations to preach at other churches?

I replied, "Yes."

Do you get revivals?

I replied, "Yes."

Does your church give you good anniversaries?

I replied, "Yes."

This reasoning salved my ego. I recognized that while I couldn't emotionally move people, I was effective. This gave me comfort and allowed me to focus on my strengths. One thing I was good at was bringing people together and sharing power. I could be radical in this regard. I once suggested to Jones that instead of building the $700,000 and $300,000 sanctuaries he and I had planned for our respective churches, we should pool our resources and build a million-dollar facility. Since his church founded mine, I told him that it was only fitting that he should be the head pastor, and I would be his assistant. Jokingly, I added that this would allow me to preach the fifty-one Sundays when he would be away. I started talking to my deacons about the idea, and when Jones saw that I was serious, he came to me and said, "Little nigga, I ain't gon' let you take my church!"

Unfortunately, he died without having fulfilled his vision, and I was at Mount Canaan for fifty-two years and didn't fulfilled mine. Imagine what we could've done together!

We must figure out how to work together. There is no tradition more associated with black churches than "splits." One faction in a church breaks off to become the "New" or "Greater" or "Number 2" version of the old church. Likewise, our organizations splinter, adopting some variation of the original organization's name. There is nothing great about any of this, and we must strive to do better.

KNOW YOUR GIFTS

I t was a great breakthrough to realize preaching wasn't my gift. Don't get me wrong. I can deliver a powerful sermon, but I'm more a teacher. Once I embraced this revelation, my ministry really began to soar.

Besides, the same was true when I started to move in my other gifts. I became popular as a coalition builder and administrator. Winning office is easy; governing is hard. God gifted me in this regard, as I have a spiritual green thumb, which has allowed every church and every denominational body I was privileged to lead to flourish.

One possible reason for this success is that I don't mind sharing or relinquishing power. For example, when I first ran for president of the Louisiana Baptist Convention, I knew my opponent, Dr. Charles T. Smith, Pastor of the Shiloh Baptist Church in Baton Rouge, Louisiana, to be a gracious man and an exceptional leader. I knew that if I didn't embrace him, I risked factions sprouting, which could split the convention. I chose him to be one of my vice presidents; since, he had leverage and also because I felt he was qualified, more so even than I was.

I always felt a bit guilty about being president. Before he died, I went to him and apologized for even getting in the race. He took the high ground until the end, telling me I had proven a smart and wise leader. He made me understand that though he was more qualified on paper, the folks chose me, and that being a unifier, was its own kind of genius. I kept the state convention from splitting during my tenure. I view this as Dr. Smith also viewed it, as one of my greatest professional accomplishments.

HONOR THE ELDERS AND LOVE THE BABIES

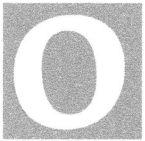

Older members have influence. They have earned the right to be trusted. They've been through it. They have built relationships. Remember, they have children, grandchildren, and friends in the church. They generally have far more influence than a new pastor. Rather than work against them, get them to work with you. A friend once told me about a particular elder who was combative. Rather than trying to fight the woman or keep her from fighting others, he befriended her and enlisted her to fight his battles. It worked perfectly.

When older members find it difficult to accept a young pastor and a new direction, it's easy to visualize these senior members as obstacles. I know this because I did. Yet the longer I served at our church, the better both the longtime members and I got at supporting each other. In the early years, I thought I was the patient one. As time went on, though, I realized just how patient they were with me as a young and growing pastor.

The Bible says so much about honoring our elders. I've been fortunate to have the opportunity to do so in all my churches, especially the second church I pastored, which was filled with elder saints. Two had been members for ninety years, and many for eighty years. Therefore, I went in honoring those matriarchs and patriarchs. At another of my churches, there was this reverend who was always named by the community, so I venerated him including the people who were baptized and taught by him, and I established a day for them to honor his name. Though none of the twelve deacons at my second church, "New Boggy" voted for me, we became the best of friends, and they became my strongest allies. The only way any left me was by death and then I preached at their funerals. When the people saw how I treated their grandparents and great-grands, they embraced me.

The reason I chose to cherish and value church elders was the wisdom they held, but I noticed that when one holds seniors and children in high regards, everybody who knows them will show support. I initially saw this with children, especially at the "The Easter program." Everyone, including the daddy who never comes to the afternoon service, will be there. It won me admiration I would not have otherwise received.

In addition to this, if a pastor loves the people whom his members love, like their parents and children, he will gain the love of the whole church.

DON'T
BELITTLE MEN

Dr. Jemison was not only a great denominational leader, in my opinion, he was the father of the modern day civil rights movement. Dr. King visited him in Baton Rouge to seek his counsel on how he successfully organized a bus boycott in Baton Rouge. Subsequently, Dr. King modeled the Montgomery Boycott from the pattern set forth by Dr. Jemison. Dr. Jemison could be supportive. He groomed me to become his successor for the Louisiana Missionary Baptist State convention.

Dr. T. J. Jemison was a formidable and brilliant man, but he had one shortcoming, and it was the real reason ministers pushed for his ouster as president of the Louisiana State Baptist Convention. His peers, which he thought didn't exist, felt he treated them like boys. This troubled Jemison when he heard it. Since he held men in such high regard, the rumor hurt him deeply, and he was so depressed by the revelation that he agreed to step down without a fight.

Other pastors have been guilty of talking down to men. I've observed pastors demeaning men from the sacred space of the pulpit when those in the pew can't defend themselves. I've heard them say things like, "You can't depend on men" or "Men ain't no good." I've observed the hurt in men's eyes. This gave me an understanding of why men leave the church.

If one says a person is no good, he'll try to live down to that expectation.

Pastors must stop castigating men by suggesting men can't be trusted and won't make decent husbands. It is a pastor's responsibility to make sure the men in his fold are taught to be responsible, qualified husbands and men.

One way I did this was to hold a class for men only. Before Sunday school, I used to meet with all the men and we studied how to be godly men. On those Sundays, we would have a room packed with men eager to be better, to be great. We would fellowship in class and socialize outside of the church. There are men who will testify that this experience changed their lives. This one, I believe, deserves replication.

DON'T
TRY TO DO
EVERYTHING
AT ONCE

hen I was growing up, our school schedule revolved around the times when we were needed in the fields. In the spring, once the threat of frost had passed, we would start working the soil by digging long narrow trenches with a hoe or plow. Afterwards, we would run water over them to get the soil nice and moist and then plant seeds in groups of three, a few inches apart. When the seeds were covered, and the soil firmed, we'd go back to school and wait.

In a good year, the germination process would happen fast. In a week's time, we'd start to see sprouts. We wouldn't have to do much over the summer but water them. In a month's time, the plants would start branching. Another month would have those branches covered in squares, the flower buds. Seemingly overnight, the fields would be covered in white flowers.

Once the wind and bees were done with their business, the flowers would turn pink; then just as suddenly, they'd start to darken. Within a week, that flower would've shriveled up and fallen off. At this point, the cotton bolls would start to show. They grew over the course of a month or more. During this time, all we could really do was pray there would be no drought or flood. When the bolls cracked open, the fluffy white fiber would appear, and it would be time to pick the cotton.

Three things I learned from picking cotton: Harvesting is the hardest part, a picker can be cut while picking, and one cannot pick all the cotton at once.

The same is true of the work the church does. There is nothing more exciting than a pastor on fire for the Lord! Ministers want to ensure a good harvest, but I learned from working the plantation fields, one does not do everything or save everybody at once. This waiting is what I made sure to do whenever I came to pastor a new church. At first, I needed to see what it would take and what the people wanted. A pastor has to do the early toiling and then be patient. If not, one ends up picking the flowers when the best fruit is yet to come. Some of the work of the church will fall away, but remember, it's just making room for the big harvest.

Besides, a pastor also needs to know how to steer the church. On the plantation, sometimes, I had to plow with the mules. I agreed to do it, but I was determined not to do that mule talk: "whoa" for stop, "getty up" for go, and so forth. I said to myself, "I'm going to speak to the mule in my language," so I'd say, "Go ahead," and pop the reins; "Stop," and pull both reins; "To the right," and pull the reins to the right.

So, what I discovered was it wasn't the words, it was the pull of the reins that moved the mules. The church is the same way. The head must know how to direct the body.

Let me put it another way. People say one can lead a horse to water but not make him drink, but my daddy would say, "You put enough salt in his diet, which will make him thirsty, and he'll find water on his own." Therefore, when I have something I want the church to do; I first give them the salt and eventually raise their thirst for it.

MODELING
SCRIPTURE
RATHER
THAN OTHER
CHURCHES

he pastor is the shepherd, and, as such, is responsible for the practices of the flock. My goal has always been to teach the church what is Biblical. To do this, however, we must KNOW the Bible. Too often, we don't understand the scriptures. For example, a sick person will claim good health by quoting the scripture, "By his stripes I am healed," but in that context, the Bible is not talking about physical illness. It refers to healing from sins, not physical ailments. It is not our physical, but our spiritual healing that comes from what happened on the cross.

Hence, it is the pastor's responsibility to correct false notions and behaviors carried out in the church. I never asked my congregation to do anything that was not taught in Scripture. Everything we do or signed up to do has to have a biblical basis. If the Scripture does not mandate it or model it, then we should question if we should be doing it.

When a pastor recognizes that a church tradition has no biblical basis, he must answer this question: "Is this practice in contradiction with the Bible?" If yes, it must be dealt with immediately. Such an issue arose at New Boggy, which for generations benefited from oil and gas production revenue. Because they were afforded a financial independence rare among black churches, tithing was never emphasized. When I arrived, that income was dwindling. God mandated that His people give to Him a tithe, ten percent, so whether or not the church needed the money, the members needed to be following the Word.

Sometimes our traditions are not in conflict with the Bible but are rooted in culture or tradition that is no longer applicable. For example, Lake Bethlehem only had two Sunday services a month when I began pastoring them. New Boggy was the first rural church to go full time, and Lake Bethlehem was the first church in the Cooper Road community to become full time. What I did was to employ skill and strategy, which is a proven method to lead the church to change.

Another tradition we needed to reconsider was tying a scarf around the head of those just baptized. The issue first came up in the 1970s when afros were popular and then again in the 1980s when Jheri curls became fashionable. The handkerchief wasn't conducive to the hairstyles women and men were wearing. We insisted on tying the handkerchief even though it was not adding anything, and I still don't know why we did it, but it took me fifty years to get them to change.

There is another ageless tradition it has taken me fifty years to deal with. Why do we cover the communion trays with a tablecloth? No one could answer me. I explained that churches started this. Ideally, the table should be exposed; however, in our rural churches, we had the windows up for air circulation. We were trying to protect the communion elements from the flies.

Covering the communion was not going to send anyone to hell, so I never created hell in the church over that issue.

Conversely, we resist new things because we haven't done them that way. Folks didn't want drums or praise dancing in the church. Ironically, this is actually Biblical. We must always consult the operations manual. We pick up from others what can be or is sometimes false doctrine, but because others say it and practice it, we adopt it without examining it.

I used to say, "Before I die, I want to pastor a church of God." They thought I meant another denomination, but I meant a church doing what God instructs. I wanted a church that was Biblically astute.

PREPARE FOR RETIREMENT

Too often, Baptist pastors only leave a church when they are voted out, run out, or rolled out. When they leave voluntarily, it is usually to pastor another congregation.

When I was growing up in the church, retirement of preachers was not practiced. They modeled what they thought was the Moses pattern. Prophets died as prophets. Besides, a church felt so obligated to its pastor that it would not consider retiring him.

At every stage of my life, I was prudent enough to know when it was time to transition. I didn't want this to be any different. Age alone is not the reason I'm retiring. I believe older pastors serve a purpose. There is great balance in the young and old working together. The one needs the other, but I am old. I have seen it all and done plenty. I have experience, but after sixty-two years preaching ministry and sixty as a pastor, I don't have the energy to do things required of a pastor.

Five years prior to my retirement I began to prepare Mount Canaan. I gave them my five-year transition plan; however, several decades ago, I began preparing to have a retirement income. The lack of retirement income remains the reason many pastors are unable to retire. Social Security benefits were not an option for many clergymen who were not part of the Social Security payment system, but even my rural churches paid my portion of Social Security taxes from which I receive benefits today.

I was at Mount Canaan fifteen years before they considered giving me a retirement or a car allowance. I taught them what the Bible said on how to care for a pastor and they received it. Eventually, they put me in a very handsome retirement fund that allows me to continue to receive an amount equivalent to my salary.

I also wanted to make sure I left Mount Canaan in a good position and turn over to my successor a thriving, well-oiled church. Together with the deacons and other church leaders, we looked at every aspect of the church, our programs, services, and of course, our finances. We looked at our mission and evaluated where we were. We examined each to learn what was working, what was failing, what needed to be tweaked or ended. We did surveys that were very revealing. For example, we learned the average age of our deacons was sixty plus. I struggled with whether I should ordain younger deacons as I was preparing to leave, but we decided it was best to add them to have a more balanced group of stewards.

We wanted to know where the potential for growth was. At times, it was a difficult, stressful, even painful process, but we came out in the end a stronger body in Christ.

Finally, the church was ready to select a successor. This was monumental, and I made sure the church and search committee were commissioned based on the Scriptures, prepared and able to search for God's choice. I am pleased with their selection because I know we did it right; therefore, God is pleased.

In my transition planning, I knew my leaving as a pastor would be a loss to Mount Canaan, but what I didn't anticipate was the death of their First Lady. They tolerated me as pastor, but they loved Norma; there is no question about it! The church is struggling now because it is forced to deal with two losses. My last lesson to the church is an unintended but necessary one, involving the celebration of the transitions of retirement and Norma's homegoing.

As for me, I am determined to trust in God's word. Rather than focusing on the loss of my love and all the things I am going to miss about Mount Canaan, my sons of the house and the young men I've mentored, I am focused on what I'll gain in retirement and what Mount Canaan will profit from a new leader. I promised Mount Canaan I'd do it in such a way that it would be celebratory.

I have to go with a bang, the celebratory bang.

LETTER TO FAMILY

My beloved family,

We have undergone a sudden change, but we are fortified, and we will make it. We are so blessed to have each other. I am so delighted to belong to you. I not only love you, but I like and admire you from the core of my heart.

Herman, dear brother, you've turned out to be a great dad, husband, and Christian. You've led by example, having devotion with your family every week. You became the priest of your household. I really admire that about you and wish I could emulate you. I'm a preacher in the church, but I'm not sure I have been the priest in my house. The greatest compliment you ever paid me was your saying that after Norma introduced you to your beautiful girl, you knew you'd marry her because she reminded you so much of my wife. The fact that you've all loved Norma like a sister has meant everything to me.

Brother Robert, you are the genius of our family. You didn't have to put forth any effort to master the material you were learning in high school and college. You possess an unusual ability to make friends. Really, you became the civil rights activist after me, leading your high school peers reaction to my beating.

Everywhere you go, you become a leader and people look up to you. Even after you were stricken with this heart problem and had the heart transplant. It might take you out of the public eye but not out of the heart of the public. In fact, it doesn't impede your ability to connect with people. You are the one who, of us Blakes to multiply and replenish the earth. You provided me with a whole host of nieces and nephews. Thanks, man.

Carolyn, you are my baby sister, but I've always felt I was as responsible for you as I was for my daughters. You are the smartest of us all. I'm so glad that after decades as an educator, you continue to make time to instruct me as you did your high school and college students.

Elizabeth, you are our oldest, and we so wanted to keep you close, but you got away from us. We were hoping to convince you to attend college closer to home, but when you persisted, we finally agreed to let you spread your wings. You can't imagine the fear that was in our hearts when Norma left you in Washington, D.C., to attend Howard University. Nevertheless, you made the right decision, and we are so proud of what you have accomplished. More than your career of working at the World Bank and other corporations in that area, you have a great work ethic and an ability to find solutions to problems or, at the very least, strategies for coping with them. I have no doubt you've passed this on to your children.

Chubby, Harry II, my namesake, you quite literally saved my life ten years ago when you agreed to join me in the ministry.

Who would have thought your training and experience in the Marines and Corporate America would be great preparation for managing a church? You serve your calling in a mighty way.

Rodney Earl, early on we discovered you had inherited my learning disability, dyslexia. We sought healthcare professionals who suggested we medicate you. We followed their direction, which subsequently led to your substance abuse. I failed you there in that I was unable to analyze whether the decision was best for you. It pains me to even talk about it now. I pray you can forgive me for how I have failed you. I never knew how to help you with your addictions. You were that child who required more time and attention from your father. I'm sorry I couldn't provide it, but I hope you know my love for you was always resolute. However, both your mother and I discovered and agreed you are a great child, a loving person, and perhaps the most caring person we have ever met. We concluded that if in this life we were stricken ill, you are the one of our children who would forsake all to come and give us the attention we needed in our final years. I am so very proud of the grandson you gave us, Rodney II. Your mother departed with great joy knowing you are recovering from your addiction. The fact that you have found sobriety is one of the greatest blessings I've experienced. This is what family means.

As you recall, your mother's last recorded message was to you. "Rodney, sorry I missed you. Call me back. I am home." Thank you for sharing that with me.

Monica, I can't help but smile when I think of my baby girl. I often recount the story of you rushing up to me when all the other children knew to flee, saying, "Daddy, I am not going to be afraid of you. I am going to be your friend, and you are gonna like it because you're my daddy." You have been my best buddy ever since!

The best investment I have ever made was supplementing your salary out of my own pocket to have you work at the church. You started answering my phones in elementary school and never stopped. I thought I would lose you to a company after you earned your accounting degree, but I'm so delighted you have continued to work with me and been a part of so many positive organizations—Alpha Kappa Alpha Sorority, Incorporated and the Links Incorporated among them. I'm very proud of the work you do as the general secretary of the National Baptist Congress of Christian Education for the largest black religious body in America. You've broken tradition and torn down walls. There are more people in the convention who know you than those who know me. They now say, "This is Monica's daddy."

What pleases me most is that you've put all of my grandchildren on the right track.

You have all my love.

LESSONS

CHOOSE YOUR IN-LAWS WISELY THEN TREAT THEM LIKE FAMILY

I never courted Norma. I wooed her parents instead! Nancy Gilliam Jernigan and Claude Jernigan were wonderful people. I knew I was going to marry Norma and figured her momma and daddy would see to it that she did. I knew that they were smart enough and mature enough to look at me and know that I would take care of their daughter. They would say yes when I proposed to them! Norma used to joked that I probably should've married them!

I have not experienced in-law conflict. My wife's family loved me, and I loved them. My wife jokes that they treated me like I was their blood and she, the adopted daughter. My mother was a little jealous that Norma took her firstborn son, but Norma knew how to work Momma, though I don't know if she ever truly forgave Norma.

Norma's three younger siblings, Christell, James Howard, and Claude Ester, also treated me as if I was there brother and assisted in my conquest of Norma, especially, James Howard! From the moment Norma entered my life, my family doubled.

Throughout our marriage, Norma and I clung to our extended family. At points, we've lived together and of course, we would always spend vacations and holidays together. I have made sure to embrace the spouses of my children in this very same way. We are all stronger and better together!

MARRIAGE IS
COMPROMISE

My brother Herman has helped me see how to be a good husband. He went to the military. His wife, Mary was the kind of woman who supported anything her husband chose to do. They both finished college and then got married. They've grown up together. They have four children who support each other. Herman is a godly man who showed his children how to be a man and how a man ought to treat his wife and children. He and his wife were in harmony from the beginning. This was the case for Norma and me on most issues, but there was one in which we moved in opposite directions.

I was of the view that Norma should stay at home with the children, but she insisted she wanted to work outside the home. Norma had grown up in a family with a strong work ethics, and she felt she needed to work outside of the home to live up to the standard her family had set. She also thought a career would give her confidence and make her feel good about herself, and she liked the idea of having her own money. This was a struggle for me because my mom had always been at home with her children, and we loved having her home. This was all I knew.

Norma and I wrestled with this for some time as I was adamant, my wife should not work. This frustrated Norma and I believe her unhappiness manifested itself in physical illnesses and asthma. I grieved with her and gave my assent. Finally, I just said, "Okay, go to work."

With my blessing, Norma got a job at AT&T, raised four children, managed a house, and never had another asthma attack.

I was lucky to have married my soulmate, a woman who shared most of my views; however, learning to compromise was essential for my marriage and life.

LEARN HOW TO MEET YOUR SPOUSE'S NEEDS

My mother loved my daddy, who was a good husband in that he was kind to and provided for us. He didn't walk around saying "I love you," but his actions showed us that he did. I thought all I needed to do to be a good husband was do what I saw my daddy do, but that's not how marriage works. One must learn how to treat a spouse.

Early on in our marriage, I failed quite a lot. I was failing sometimes and didn't even realized it. For example, one day, after our children were grown and we even had grandkids, Norma reminded me of how I used to scold her on Sunday mornings early in our marriage when we only had one car. She mimicked how I used to say, "Norma, if you aren't ready to go to church when I am, I'm going to leave you because I'm not going to let anything come between me and God."

But what I failed to see (and she was now pointing out) was that Norma wasn't trying to come between me and God. She explained, "However, you didn't realize that I had to bathe and dress your half of the children, make your half of the bed, and cook your half of the meal. And all you did was prepare yourself."

Norma was carrying my load and hers, and I never realized it. Revelations like this, led me on a quest to figure out how to meet my spouse's needs. Of course, the first place I looked was the Bible. What I discovered was how important family is to God, who created the family before he created the church. The first miracle Jesus performed was not at a church but at a home at a wedding. This revelation freed me to make my wife and family priorities.

This was just the beginning of the process of learning to be a good spouse. I found other texts and self help books were useful to me as well. Another thing that helped was coming together with other men. This fellowship and common quest for a good marriage helped the men in our church enormously.

I sought to equip the men to meet their wives needs. My strategy was to have the men meet with me on a Sunday morning to equip them to become the best husbands for their wives. We used the Bible as our basis for the curriculum. We would hear from men who had successful marriages, but the thing that helped us all the most was hearing from wives in successful marriages.

It was an Aha! moment for me. I realized a spouse needs a person of the opposite sex to provide perspective. I came to rely on the advice of my dear friend, Mrs. Angenetta Lott. I feel she raised me for my wife.

I believe every spouse should have some friends of the opposite sex to advise them. I've taught my children, my male sons, they ought to have at least one female friend in their lives because a female friend can teach them how to have a good relationship and be the husbands their wives want. The same is true for my daughters regarding male friends. It is great that we have our marriage partnerships, but friendships are important, perhaps even imperative to maintaining a good marriage. I hold friendship in high esteem, almost next to salvation, I think. I really value friendship!

BE THERE
FOR YOUR
CHILDREN

Children, learn from my mistakes. I wasn't as good a father to you as mine was to me. I believe the proof of this is in the pudding. My daddy had no formal education, couldn't read, and was very poor, but all four of his children were college graduates. In spite of how much more I could offer, one of my own didn't even finish high school. What accounts for this difference? Certainly not aptitude, for you are all brilliant. I believe it was the confidence and security Daddy's mere presence poured into us. Conversely, I was seldom home, and when I was, I was too busy for you. I don't beat myself up about it. I live with it. Nevertheless, I accept the truth of it.

I was doing revival in Atlanta, Georgia, at a church where the daughter of Dr. King, Bernice was a member; we were in the pastor's study, and I remarked how wonderful Dr. King was to which she replied, "Y'all always say my daddy was great, but he was nothing to us. He was never there." It was an awakening moment for me. I saw myself having been a father in the house and absent emotionally and in other ways. Indeed, really disconnected from the children.

I was so busy helping other people's children that I didn't have the kind of involvement that I should have had with my own. I'm sure I missed out on a lot of bonding with them and understanding their needs. We, of course, spent time together, even without their mother. We went on trips to major cities and areas with historical significance. Especially, the day to day being there listening to them was something I missed.

My wife replicated my mother, making me king of the house. My youngest, Monica, broke the mold. She brought me down off my pedestal. She said, "Why are we running? Daddy, I ain't scared of you. You are gonna be my friend and like it!"

Spanking was the slavery method of punishment, and that's all we knew and used on our children to get their attention.

Daddy spanked me one time. My momma never hit me. It's not true that we need to hit our children. Hitting is often a substitute for patience or an act of frustration.

I remember my parents had bought a radio, and I was at home alone. I opened the back of the radio. It had this little guy that controlled the stations, a string, and two wheels. I pulled the string off the wheel. My daddy put the string back on the wheel and never asked me about it.

Although I do believe in discipline, but I don't believe there needs to be whipping. It's all we knew, so we passed it on to our children to get their attention.

I think being there for your children means going to the school on parents night, helping them with their homework. Parents must show up during the school days. Doing everyday things that children like to do. My daddy and I worked together, sawing wood. But I recall and relish those moments when we were together. Whether it is something fun or otherwise, they relish being together.

I read a story once where a dad and his son went fishing together. The boy said it rained, it turned cold, we didn't catch a single fish, but it was the best day I ever had. The daddy's perspective was ...worst day I ever had. The child's perspective was associated with the spending of a quality time with him.

There is a bit of childlikeness that we never shed. Even when we become grown and old, we need the presence and touch of our parents. I'm almost ninety years old, and I just delight in thinking about being with my daddy even after my mother had passed. Even if we weren't talking, it was nice. You never outgrow the need for your parent's touch.

As an adult I listened to my parents' counsel, not orchestrated but just talking. Their advice has helped me tremendously. As a parent, I've taught myself to listen to my children and wait for them to solicit my advice. It is at those moments that I've shared the wisdom of my mistakes and my successes. As a matter of fact, I found myself doing the same thing with my grandchildren. My grands tend to relish talks with me. All of my grandsons come and sit and talk with me.

They ask, "Granddaddy, how do you do this?" or "What do you think about that?" It means everything to me that I am able to be there for them.

WE ARE RESPONSIBLE FOR EACH OTHER

It is imperative that the family be there for one another at every occasion and not just when it is convenient. When my father got older and could no longer live alone, he came to stay with me, as I was the oldest and still living in Shreveport. It was not his fault that I was born male. It was still my responsibility. Most times, men do not take the kind of responsibility for the aging or ill parents as they should, but I felt it incumbent upon me, not my wife or my younger siblings, to care for him.

He said to me one day, "Why don't you do for me what's best? Take me to one of those aging facilities. You can still care for me, and I'll be around people of my own age, I can relate to. I don't want to be a burden." That was unusual. Usually, older people want to die in their homes. He went to the home and lived another ten years. But until the day he closed his eyes, he knew he could count on me.

Sometimes, a family member goes through something difficult and needs our support.

Harry wanted to be in the Secret Services, but his wife didn't want to move. He wanted to build a house, but she wanted to buy an already built one. He felt he was always the one who had to sacrifice and give in, and he was bitter. He felt defeated.

"Daddy, I will kill her and walk over her as though I've killed an animal."

He was an ex-marine, taught to kill, and no one de-programmed him, so this was serious.

I called a family meeting and said, "I don't want to lose a daughter-in-law, but I certainly don't want to lose her and my son. We have got to save Chubby."

Chubby's crisis was largely emotional, but our other son, Rodney, needed us emotionally and in other ways after his wife was killed in a car wreck. A while later, his son came down with lymphoma. Norma and I put everything aside to care for him.

Our grandson recovered, went to college and got a degree in engineering. My grandson turned into a very good man, and I am just grateful that he allowed me to be there for him.

We don't often think of it this way, but it is also our responsibility to allow our family to be there for one another. My sister experienced physical abuse. We never knew about it. She didn't want the family to know she chose a man who abused her. I felt it reflected poorly on me that I couldn't detect he was violent. I hate it that she suffered silently, and I wasn't able to protect her.

Just as it's important for the family to be there for each other, it is equally important that family members share so their family can be there and provide for them.

HOW TO SAY GOODBYE

My children, losing a parent is a new and painful experience for you. Offspring should bury their parents, and I thank God we've been blessed in that regard. I was around fifty and still considered myself a young man when my momma died.

Miss Doll always said she didn't want to live beyond Daddy, and when he suffered a stroke, she hopped up and died. Daddy got better and lived another fifteen years! I laugh thinking of how shocked and disappointed she must've been to wake in heaven and realize Daddy had pulled one over on her. At least, this is the way I tell it.

Momma had been diagnosed with brain cancer. Daddy was recuperating at my home. He'd already gone to sleep when the hospital called and said Momma had passed. I figured there was nothing either of us could do, as Miss Doll would still be dead in the morning, so I waited and told Daddy the next morning.

I said, "Daddy, Miss Doll died last night."

He said, "I shol' hate that," then had his breakfast.

My daddy grieved over my mother's death but didn't allow it to stop him from living or loving us. I was determined to model that with Momma and again when Daddy passed away. Day to day, I focus on the happy times. I encouraged myself to do that by pouring out the sad things from my mind and focusing on the happy times. It's like having one glass and the choice to drink water or wine. I have to pour one out to drink the other.

Naturally, sometimes the grief overwhelmed me. When that would happen, I'd go to my safe deposit box where I keep my most valued possessions and remove the knit cap daddy slept in and the money rag momma used to keep in her bosom. I then close myself up in a room and cry until my eyes run out of tears. When I was done, I'd change the channel so to speak, and go back out into the world and keep on living.

This process has three parts. The first, our family is exceptionally good at: love each other while we're here. Express it; demonstrate it. Too often people wait until their loved ones are gone to love them. I'm so thankful to God he revealed to me before it was too late that I couldn't neglect my family for the ministry or anything else. Norma and I got to have so many wonderful times together, and during her last weeks, our family spent every moment with her. In this way, we modeled David who during the time his child was sick, did nothing but fast and pray for healing. However, when he saw the servants grieving together, he asked, "Is the child dead?"

After the servants answered yes, David got up, bathed, ate, and worshipped. He explained to his puzzled servants that he did all he could while his child lived, "But now that the baby is dead, why should I fast? I can't bring him back to life. Someday I will go to be with him, but he cannot come back to me."

This approach to death is repeated several times in the bible. I believe the lesson for us is to do what we can for our loved ones while they live then release them to die. Let them go.

I taught my members to give their loved ones permission to die. I've had many members share testimony regarding this. One deacon said, he went to his wife's bedside and said, "I love you dearly, but you have permission to do what you please, live or die." Three minutes later, she died. I don't believe it is a coincidence that both my parents died while I was away from the hospital.

Once we "loose" them as the Word intends, we can complete the final stage, which is to celebrate their departure and look forward to being reunited with them.

The celebration should begin with the funeral. Of course, you are still hurting and adjusting to life without your loved one, in order to have a joyous homegoing, the funeral must be planned in this manner. I like to open a funeral with 90 seconds of pew greeting and fellowship. After all, funerals make some of the best reunions! Upbeat music must be decided on in advance. I enjoy the plantation melodies, "Jesus is on the main Line" and "Glory, Glory, Since I laid My Burdens Down." Who is going to hear those tunes and not clap for joy? The minister's sermon should keep to the tone. The preacher who did Norma's wake had the theme, "Once, Twice, Three Times a Lady." It was glorious and a perfect tribute to Norma. I loved it.

LETTER TO
NORMA

y dearest Norma,

I smile each time I catch a glimpse of your portrait in the hall outside of what was intended to be our master bedroom in our new home. I greet you, "Hey, girl."

You never asked for anything, certainly not a new house. But I listened to you, and every time we passed the house, you would say, "Oh, look. It is still for sale."

After we closed on it, your friend, Margie told me you said, "I never thought my husband would buy that house!" It was so nice to know I could still surprise you!

I thought about not moving in, but the children wanted me here so that I was closer to them. I'm glad we got to make a few memories together here. I laugh every time I look out at the lake remembering the first time we fished on our pier, you were still wearing the St. John knit skirt you had worn to church. Even though I insisted it was getting dark and time to go, you won by simply saying you weren't ready to leave.

The children found your father's pocket watch had it repaired and gave it to me. It has an extra special meaning to me and I hold it daily because it helps me to feel your presence. Eventually, I'll place your scarf in the safe deposit box where it will reside with Momma's handkerchief and Daddy's knit nightcap. When I need to I will take it out, go to a private room and cry my eyes out for as long as I need to. When I'm done I'll dry my eyes and come out and nobody will be the wiser.

I owe everything to you, my dear, especially the words you spoke on our 50th anniversary.

"I have been a Married Widow for 50 Years," she said.

Your words broke my heart because I knew they were true; I knew that I had done you, our children, and the rest of our family a grave injustice by neglecting you. I justified it in my mind by believing the Civil Right Movement and the needs of the church were greater, but maturity brought me to realize they were not. Maybe, I was too close to see your suffering and to see your pain. I was so focused on the outside world.

Because of your words, I knew I had a full decade to make up to you. We had good times throughout our sixty years, but for those last ten, I was intentional.

From the bottom of my heart, I thank you for all you did to make my life possible. While I was out trying to save the world, you saved our family. You raised the kids, tended the home, supported me, and worked outside the home. You did it all with grace and love. I often remarked, "My wife doesn't have a degree but is smarter by accident than everyone in the room."

You never wanted to be out front. You wanted your husband to lead, but I was only able to lead others because I had your support. I remember after I was badly beaten by police after the Little Union memorial, you stayed with me. You gave the children to some others, and you focused on nursing me. That night you held my head in your lap, nursed me, and made sure I got the care and attention I needed. Because of your skepticism, you had me flown to Dallas, Texas to doctors and I spent four weeks in Dallas recovering with you.

They say your home is where your heart is and your heart was always with me. I was looking forward to spending our days and nights sitting on the patio watching sunrises and sunsets. My greatest comfort is knowing that you knew how much I loved you.

Eternally yours,
Harry

Acknowledgements

I would like to first thank my daughter, Monica Blake Mickle, without whom this book would not have become a reality. I would also like to thank my editor, Yolanda Young, who shepherded me through the arduous writing process. The end product made the journey worthwhile.

www.ingramcontent.com/pod-product-compliance
Lightning Source LLC
Chambersburg PA
CBHW021824090426
42811CB00032B/2016/J